It Happened In West Virginia

It Happened In Series

It Happened In West Virginia

Remarkable Events That Shaped History

Rick Steelhammer

Guilford, Connecticut

Copyright © 2013 by Morris Book Publishing, LLC

Editor: Tracee Williams
Project Editor: Lauren Brancato
Layout: Justin Marciano
Map: Melissa Baker © Morris Book Publishing, LLC

Library of Congress Cataloging-in-Publication Data

Steelhammer, Rick.
 It happened in West Virginia : remarkable events that shaped history /
Rick Steelhammer.
     pages cm — (It happened in series)
 Includes bibliographical references and index.
 ISBN 978-0-7627-7054-0
 1. West Virginia—History—Anecdotes. I. Title.
 F241.6.S74 2010
 975.4—dc23
                                                    2012044060

Printed in the United States of America

10 9 8 7 6 5 4 3 2 1

CONTENTS

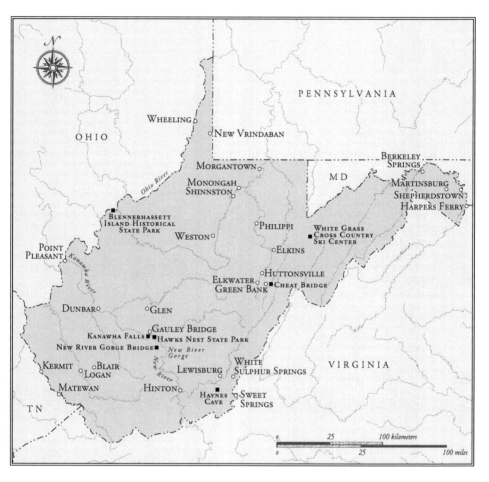

WEST VIRGINIA

CONTENTS

ACKNOWLEDGMENTS

While writing a book is, for the most part, a solitary undertaking, doing the research needed to drive the writing sometimes requires help. I received it in abundance from David Schau, Elizabeth Fraser, and Olivia Bravo at the Kanawha County Public Library, from Joe Geiger and Terry Lowry at West Virginia Archives and History, and from author/historian W. Hunter Lesser with the Rich Mountain Battlefield Foundation.

For encouraging my writing and forgiving my many absences to accomplish it during the past two years, a special thanks is due to my wife, Pam. This one's for you.

INTRODUCTION

Passions run deep in this state of peaceful hills and hollows.

You don't have to dig deep into West Virginia's history to find stories of war and insurrection, justice and oppression.

In the only state completely encompassed by the Appalachian mountain range, thunder has frequently echoed across our slopes—but it has not always been the product of lightning.

West Virginia is the only state spawned by the Civil War, thanks to the efforts of political leaders in northern and western counties who took issue with Virginia's vote to secede from the Union. Overall, public sentiment in the land that was to become the thirty-fifth state only slightly favored the federal cause, and a number of counties were decidedly pro-Confederate. Battles, skirmishes, and raids reached every corner of the state, often putting those who were friends, neighbors, and relatives before the war on opposite sides of the killing fields.

Not long after the Civil War came to an end, gunfire echoed across the Tug Fork Valley, where the Hatfield and McCoy families were ramping up their infamous feud along the West Virginia–Kentucky border.

By the early twentieth century, explosions caused by gas and dust accumulations in underground coal mines boomed across the mountains of West Virginia, causing hundreds of deaths. An explosion that shot through the connected Monongah No. 6 and No. 8 mines near Fairmont in 1907 left more than 360 miners dead and brought about the nation's first federal mine safety regulations. The Monongah blast remains the biggest mine disaster in United States history.

Coal miners seeking better pay and safer working conditions through unionization clashed frequently with coal operators during the early 1900s.

While union miners relied mainly on work stoppages and intimidation of strikebreakers to boost their cause, coal operators turned to strong-arm detective agencies, hired guns, machine gun-equipped locomotives, and even bomb-dropping aircraft to enforce their will.

Coalfield hostilities reached the boiling point in August of 1921, when thousands of well-armed miners marched from Kanawha County to Blair Mountain on the Boone-Logan County line, where an army of mercenaries hired by coal operators awaited them in trenches fortified with machine gun nests. The ensuing Battle of Blair Mountain is considered the largest civil insurrection since the Civil War.

While violence and bloodshed are a part of the state's past, West Virginia passion has a kinder, gentler side as well.

George Washington's love of a pristine mountain mineral spring he first visited as a youth led to the development of the nation's first public spa at Berkeley Springs.

Convinced that the northern town of Wheeling could become the gateway for the nation's westward expansion, the river town's movers and shakers sold stock and raised the money needed to build what was then the world's longest suspension bridge. The first span to cross the Ohio River, completed in 1849, is the oldest bridge of its type still in use.

Inventors and industrialists Henry Ford, Thomas Edison, and Harvey Firestone fell in love with the quiet beauty of the state's eastern mountains enough to hold car-camping adventures there in 1918 and 1921, once bringing along a United States president.

The peaceful green, rolling hills in the state's Northern Panhandle inspired an India-born Hindu swami to envision and build the nation's largest Hare Krishna community there in the 1970s.

And West Virginia's passion for the state's rugged beauty and the adventure sports it makes possible led to Bridge Day, an annual fall celebration begun in 1979. On Bridge Day, tens of thousands of people stroll across the 876-foot-high New River Gorge Bridge to take in the fall colors and sweeping views of the cliffs and rapids below, while hundreds of BASE jumpers legally parachute off the span.

More than twelve thousand years separate the Bridge Day crowds from the Paleo-Indians who first occupied West Virginia and hunted woolly mammoths and mastodons with stone-tipped spears as the second Ice Age came to an end. But I think both groups share the spirit of the state motto created in 1863 by Joseph Debar, the artist who also designed the state seal.

Debar's Latin inscription, "Montani Semper Liberi," arches across the lower half of the state seal, informing those who read it that "Mountaineers Are Always Free."

CALIFORNIA DREAMING

1671

After two weeks of riding westward from the civilization of eastern Virginia to the edge of the unexplored, unbroken series of mountains that make up the Appalachian range, Thomas Batts and Robert Fallam were out of supplies and low on energy, but brimming with optimism.

On September 14, 1671, the pair of explorers, accompanied by a Native American guide, reached a clearing atop a mountain ridge, giving them a sweeping view of the landscape to the southwest—a vista never before seen by European eyes.

To Fallam, the scene was "a curious prospect of hills like waves raised by a gentle breeze of wind rising one upon the other," he wrote in his journal.

Fallam's nautical description of the terrain must have struck a chord with his partner in exploration, who thought he could make out a sailing ship on the western horizon.

"Mr. Batts supposed he saw sayles," Fallam wrote, "but I rather think them to be white clifts."

In 1671 Virginia, Batts wasn't alone in suspecting that the Pacific Ocean, or Great South Sea, could lie just beyond the Appalachian Mountains to the west. Maps of the North American continent's interior were sketchy and speculative beyond the easternmost ridges of the Appalachians, which had yet to be penetrated by colonists like Batts, Fallam, and Abraham Wood, who commanded Fort Henry, a stockade and trading post at the falls of the Appomattox River near present-day Petersburg, Virginia.

For Wood, a fur trader, the idea that a coast with links to the Orient might be found relatively nearby was especially tantalizing. To investigate that theory, the trader commissioned frontiersmen Batts, Fallam, and Thomas Woods to cross the mountain range to the west. Their mission, Fallam wrote in the expedition journal, was to discover "the ebbing and flowing of the Waters on the other side of the Mountaines in order to [bring about] the discovery of the South Sea."

The trio left the home of Abraham Wood on September 1, 1671, accompanied by Penecute, "a great man of the Apomatack Indians," according to Fallam, to serve as guide, and Jack Weason, Wood's former servant.

After riding 120 miles during the first three days of the journey, the explorers came to a Sapony Indian village Batts and Fallam had previously visited, and were "joyfully and kindly received with firing of guns and plenty of provisions."

Two days later, they reached another Native American village on an island in the Staunton River, where Thomas Woods, "dangerously sick of the Flux," or dysentery, turned back to Wood's home at the falls of the Appomattox.

One week after their voyage began, the explorers caught their first glimpse of the foreboding mountains to the west. But they were not the first Europeans to reach that point: Just before reaching the foot of the range, they found a tree marked in charcoal with the letters "M.ANi."

By September 12, the party had reached another Indian village in a swampy area along the Roanoke River near present-day Salem, Virginia. From there they traveled west across several mountain ridges and valleys. The following day they reached the crest of an exceptionally high ridge and looked westward across an expanse of mountainous terrain that stretched past the western horizon.

"It was a pleasing tho' dreadful sight to see the mountains and hills as if piled one upon another," Fallam wrote. While descending that slope, the explorers encountered two more trees branded with the letters "M.ANi," marking the presence of the unknown explorer who preceded them.

After descending the western slope of the ridge and traveling an estimated seven miles, the Batts-Fallam party encountered "a great Run, which emptied itself into the great Northerly river." The explorers had sighted the New River, which flows northward from the mountains of Western North Carolina through Virginia and halfway through West Virginia where it merges with the Gauley River to become the Kanawha River.

From there, the explorers reached the mountaintop from which Batts thought he could see a ship on the horizon and continued their westward journey for three more days, feasting on wild turkey, grapes, and deer provided by their Indian guide. On September 17, the party sighted a "curious river like Apomatoack River," that flowed northward. They descended to the stream as it flowed through a relatively wide valley containing "very rich ground," and the remnants of a deserted Indian village.

From their Native American guide they were given to understand "that the Mohecan Indians did here formerly live," Fallam wrote.

The village could not have been abandoned for long, he added, since "we found corn stalks in the ground."

Fallam described the river as "much better and broader than expected, much like James River at Col. Staggs [near present-day Richmond], the falls much like these falls."

From varying levels of high water marks that stained boulders along the stream, the explorers believed that the river was subject to tidal flows that raised and lowered its level by about three feet. In reality, of course, the water level was rising and falling in response to rainfall volume in the watershed.

"It was ebbing water when we were here," Fallam wrote. "We set a stick by the water side but found it ebbed very slowly." But before the two Virginians had a chance to further study the river's supposed tidal patterns, they were strongly urged to move on by Penecute, who had grown anxious to return home as they were concerned about traveling on land considered the domain of other tribes, and "kept such a hollowing that we durst not stay any longer to make further trial," Fallam wrote.

Before turning back, they fired their weapons and declared the river and the abandoned village to be a part of the realm of King Charles II. Batts and Fallam branded a series of trees with marks representing Virginia Governor William Berkeley and the expedition's sponsor, Abraham Wood. They also burned a mark representing their guide, Perecute.

Two weeks later, they returned safely to Fort Henry at the falls of the Appomattox.

While historians generally agree that the Batts-Fallam party reached present day West Virginia, and were likely the first Europeans to set foot in it (with the possible exception of the mysterious "M.ANi"), there is disagreement about the location of the expedition's turnaround point.

Some historians believed the party paralleled the New River as it flowed northward, ending their journey at Kanawha Falls in what is now south central West Virginia. But in 1912, after re-examining Fallam's journal, historians Clarence Alvord and Lee Bidgood concluded that the endpoint of the journey was actually Peters Falls, near the point where the New River flows through a gap in Peters Mountain very near the present-day border of Virginia and West Virginia near Glen Lyn, Virginia.

In the 1980s, history professor Alan Briceland of Virginia Commonwealth University took a new look at the expedition route by studying the topography and geology of the area described in Fallam's account. He concluded that the explorers veered off the New River and then traveled up the Tug Fork River, ending their journey near the present-day town of Matewan in Mingo County.

Later, retired US Army Corps of Engineers archeologist Robert Maslowski theorized that the turnaround point described by Fallam more closely resembled the Guyandotte River Valley near the town of Logan in what is now Logan County. Items found in association with a Native American burial unearthed in Logan in 1979 during a utility line excavation were carbon dated back to the 1660s, making the site historically consistent with the newly abandoned village described by Fallam.

Regardless of exactly where Batts and Fallam were when they wishfully watched the waters of a West Virginia river recede with an ebbing tide, it is probably just as well that they had not, in fact, reached the great western sea.

While many West Virginians would enjoy having a Pacific coast, the nation wouldn't be the same without the Great Plains, Rocky Mountains, Great Basin, and Cascade Mountains that were eventually discovered in the remaining 2,700 miles separating the Appalachians and the Pacific.

GEORGE WASHINGTON SOAKED HERE

1748

Thoughts of a peaceful mountain spring with pools of warm, healing waters shaded by giant hardwood trees provided a measure of escape for George Washington on October 27, 1777.

British victories at the Battle of Brandywine the previous month and again in early October at Germantown wrested control of Philadelphia, then America's capital, from Washington. Now, enemy troops occupied the city, while Congress occupied temporary quarters in York, Pennsylvania. More than one displaced member of Congress was calling for Washington to relinquish command of the Continental Army for losing Philadelphia to the Redcoats.

But on this date, while writing a letter to his brother Samuel from his headquarters at Dawesfield, a stone estate house at Ambler, Pennsylvania, Washington was able to escape the grim realities of war and politics and dream of better times in a more tranquil place.

Washington had just received word that his brother-in-law, Colonel Fielding Lewis, had bought property on his behalf at the newly created site of Bath, a town being laid out around a series of mineral springs believed to contain curative powers in what is now Morgan County, West Virginia.

"I am very glad Col. Lewis purchased a lot or two for me at the Warm Springs, as it was always my intention to become a proprietor there if a town should be laid off at that place," Washington wrote to his brother.

Washington first visited the springs in 1748 at the age of sixteen during his first job as a professional surveyor, working for his neighbor and mentor, Thomas Lord Fairfax, the only resident British peer in America at the time. The month-long surveying mission took Washington across the Blue Ridge and into the wilderness for the first time.

While waiting for floodwaters on the nearby Potomac River to subside enough to cross safely, "We this day called to see ye fam'd Warm Springs," and camped at the site, Washington wrote in his diary on March 18, 1748.

Crystal clear water from the springs, nestled in a narrow, shaded valley, poured out of a mountainside at a constant seventy-four degrees and splashed through a series of rock-lined pools in which early settlers bathed and soaked. A creek formed by the springs flowed down a gentle grade to the Potomac River, about five miles downstream.

Washington revisited the springs many times over the years. In 1750 and 1751, he brought his older brother, Lawrence, who suffered from tuberculosis, to the springs in hopes that the waters would heal his condition. In 1756 and 1757, as a militia officer during the French and Indian War, he searched the woods surrounding the springs for enemy forces after receiving intelligence that they had camped in the vicinity.

During the 1760s, he visited the springs many times with his family to take the waters. By that time Warm Springs had become a frontier tourist attraction for cure-seeking colonists.

"We found of both sexes about 250 people at this place, full of all manner of diseases and complaints," Washington wrote during a visit to the springs in August of 1761. "Two or three doctors are here, but whether attending as physicians or to drink the water, I know not."

During that visit to the springs, Washington found that provisions of all kinds were available from vendors, including fine veal, beef, venison, lamb, and fowl. But there was no lodging of any kind until the 1780s, when Robert Throckmorton, a distant cousin of Washington, opened the Sign of the Liberty Pole and Flag.

By that time, the new spa town was named Bath in honor of the famed English resort of the same name and had attracted a Who's Who list of American movers and shakers. Joining the Washington brothers as lot buyers at Bath were three signers of the Declaration of Independence, four signers of the Constitution, six members of the Continental Congress, and several Revolutionary War generals.

The town of Bath flourished as a spa town after the war and into the early nineteenth century, when the town post office's name was changed to Berkeley Springs. While Bath remains the community's official name, it is better known today as Berkeley Springs.

The town of 660 is the seat of government in Morgan County and the home of six spas, including Berkeley Springs State Park, which encompasses the five famed springs in which Washington soaked. Berkeley Springs may be the only state park in the nation with Roman baths, saunas, and a staff that includes masseurs and masseuses.

Each March, Berkeley Springs hosts its annual George Washington's Bathtub Celebration, featuring historical programs, spa discounts, and art and craft exhibits.

Washington's last known visit to the spa town took place in September of 1784, when he commissioned James Rumsey, who was soon to gain regional fame for developing a steamboat prototype, to build a thirty-six-foot by twenty-four-foot house and a stable on his

Berkeley Springs property. Rumsey eventually built two structures for the property. An aide to the former president described them as "badly built and of bad timber." There is no record of Washington ever occupying them. A nephew, Bushrod Washington, bought the lot and buildings for $380 following Washington's death in 1799.

GETTING THE LEAD IN

1749

As thunder from an approaching storm echoed across the bluffs rising above both shores of the Ohio River, Captain Pierre-Joseph Celoron de Bienville, leading an armada of canoes containing 215 Frenchmen and 30 allied Native Americans, scanned the shoreline for a place to take shelter.

Rounding a bend on the frontier waterway, Celoron spotted a large river flowing into the Ohio from the south, shaded by a lush stand of mature hardwoods. He signaled his party to make for the Ohio's southern shore.

Celoron and his men had been traveling on the "Belle Riviere," or "Beautiful River," as he called the Ohio, since July 29, after departing Montreal on June 15, 1749, crossing Lake Erie, and descending the Allegheny River to its junction with the Monongahela in present-day Pittsburgh. The confluence of the two rivers marks the head of the Ohio River, down which Celoron had been ordered to travel by the Marquis de la Galissoniere, the governor general of New France and the highest-ranking French official in North America.

Celoron's mission was twofold: to rekindle old alliances and trade partnerships with Native Americans in the vast Ohio River watershed, and to drive out any British traders or settlers found in the area.

King George's War, the four-year British blockade of France's North American colonies, had been over for less than one year. The French living in Canada needed to reestablish a trading presence in the Ohio country to bolster their claim for the territory, which was also claimed by England.

According to Father Bonnecamp, a Jesuit priest who accompanied Celoron, the "Beautiful River had become so little known to the French, and, unfortunately, too well known to the English" as a result of the recently ended blockade.

In addition to carrying trade goods, provisions, camping gear, and firearms, Celoron's canoes carried a number of lead plates that were to be buried near the sites where major tributary streams flowed into the Ohio. Wording inscribed on the plates claimed the surrounding land for King Louis XV of France. The practice of burying metal plates at key landmarks to claim land ownership was once common in Europe.

After burying two of the eleven-inch-long, seven-and-a-half-inch-wide lead plates at landmarks along the Allegheny River in what is now Pennsylvania, Celoron began his descent of the Ohio, crossing into present-day West Virginia waters on August 12. On that date, he encountered four Englishmen traveling in two upstream-bound pirogues, or wooden cargo boats, that were "laden with packages," he wrote in his logbook. Celoron attempted to warn the English traders away from what he claimed was French territory, but went on to note that the Englishmen "did not know how to speak French or Iroquois, which was the only language of which I had an interpreter."

Not being able to communicate with the foreigners, Celoron shrugged his shoulders, let them pass, and began scanning the glades adjacent to the river for buffalo, which he had been told were in the area.

The first lead plate burial site along the Ohio River was identified the following day, at what is believed to be the mouth of Wheeling Creek, in present-day Wheeling, now the largest town in West Virginia's Northern Panhandle. No remnants of that plate, or an iron sheath bearing a French coat of arms placed on a nearby tree, have ever been found at the site. But judging from Celoron's description of the location and its listed distance from other landmarks encountered on the journey, it was the north shore of Wheeling Creek, at the site where Fort Henry would be built twenty-five years later.

During a ceremony accompanying the burial of the property marker, Celoron used an approximation of the Native American name for the stream in recording the site, which he described as the mouth of "the river Kanououara."

On August 15, Celoron's party reached the mouth of the Muskingum River on the north bank of the Ohio, at the site of what is now Marietta, Ohio, and buried a fourth lead plate there. Fifty years later, a group of boys swimming at the confluence of the two streams discovered the plate. They used a pole to pry it from the stream bank, and upon holding the relic and feeling its weight, recognized it as a ready source of lead, while failing to recognize its historic significance.

The youths pared off a portion of the plate and began melting it, placing the molten lead in molds to create bullets. A neighbor quickly determined that the plate was engraved with French letters and must be of historic value. He stopped the boys from further recycling the artifact and arranged to have it sent to a museum in Massachusetts for safekeeping.

By August 18, Celoron and his men—eight officers, six cadets, one armorer, twenty soldiers, 150 French Canadian recruits, thirty

Iroquois, and one priest—had traveled nearly sixty miles downriver when they heard the rumble of thunder and spotted the large north-flowing river entering the Ohio.

After beaching their canoes on the south shore of the "Beautiful River" at about noon, Celoron and his men set up camp under a canopy of virgin forest while waiting out a downpour. When the rain began to break, the Frenchmen began looking for a suitable place in which to bury a fifth plate.

The large tributary stream entering the Ohio at this point turned out to be the Kanawha River, which begins at the confluence of the New and Gauley rivers at present-day Gauley Bridge and flows through Charleston before entering the Ohio at what is now Point Pleasant. According to his log, Celoron knew something about the north-flowing stream.

"This river bears canoes for forty leagues without meeting rapids, and takes its rise in Carolina," he wrote. "The English of that government come that way to ply their trade on the Beautiful River."

Celoron was correct in that shoals, rather than rapids, posed the main obstacles that greeted canoeists traveling between Point Pleasant and Kanawha Falls at Glen Ferris, more than eighty miles to the south. A "league" as described by Celoron on his voyage was the equivalent of slightly more than two miles. The French captain was also correct in his statement regarding the Kanawha's source, since its main tributary—the New River—begins near present-day Blowing Rock, North Carolina.

While the stream was known in one Native American dialect as the "Kenawha," or the river of the woods, Father Bonnecamp relied on an alternative dialect to come up with "Chinodahichetha," the stream name engraved on the plate, which they buried near the foot of a huge elm tree. The plate was buried along the eastern shore of the Kanawha, and an iron sheath bearing the coat of arms of King Louis XV was secured to the elm.

During the burial ceremony, Celoron gathered his officers and had them sign and date a copy of the inscription engraved on the plate. Translated from the French, the inscription read:

In the year 1749, we, Celoron, Knight of the Royal and Military Order of St. Louis, captain, commanding a detachment sent by the orders of Monsieur the Marquis de la Galissonierre, governor-general of Canada; upon the Beautiful River, otherwise called L'Oyo [the Ohio], accompanied by the principal officers of our detachment, have buried at the foot of an elm tree, upon the southern bank of L'Oyo, and the eastern bank Chinodaista, a leaden plate, and have attached to a tree in the same spot the arms of the King. In testimony whereof, we have drawn up the present official statement which we have signed along with Messrs. the officers at our camp, the 18th of August, 1749.

It rained so hard on the night following the ceremony that members of the French expedition had to move their camp to higher ground, and spent all of August 19 hunkered down in their shelters, waiting for the storm to break. They shoved off the following day and continued downstream for several days, making their final stop on the Ohio at the mouth of the Scioto River at what is now Portsmouth, Ohio.

There they buried a sixth and final plate, and encountered large numbers of Indians, as well as several English traders, whom they ordered to leave.

While the English wisely chose not to outwardly defy the much larger French force, Father Bonnecamp, at least, was aware that the Celoron expedition's impact on the foreigners was minimal. After the

English were told to leave the territory, "they firmly resolved to do nothing of the kind as soon as our backs were turned," the priest wrote.

Celoron's five-month journey into the Ohio frontier proved to be too little, too late, to restore French dominance in the area.

While some French traders did return to the Ohio country, the English foothold there was too strong to dislodge, as made apparent by the English victory in the seven-year French and Indian War, which broke out in 1756. The 1763 Treaty of Paris ceded control of the Ohio country to England.

Native Americans in the region, however, did not all recognize English rights to the territory.

In 1774, twenty-five years after Celoron's party broke camp at the mouth of the Kanawha, more than one thousand Virginia militiamen and a like number of Shawnee and Mingo warriors clashed at the site in the bloody Battle of Point Pleasant, an engagement narrowly won by the Virginians.

In 1846, three boys combing the east bank of the Kanawha looking for rocks to use as weights for their fishing lines saw Celoron's lead plate sticking out from the muck of the riverbank near the roots of an elm tree. They dislodged the plate and brought it to the home of an uncle of one of the boys, who in turn took it to the home of a Point Pleasant schoolteacher, who was able to partially interpret the inscription and grasp its significance.

James Laidley, who represented Kanawha County in the Virginia Assembly during the 1850s, brought the engraved lead plate to the Virginia Historical Society Museum in Richmond.

Of the six lead plates buried during the Celoron expedition, only the Marietta and Point Pleasant plates have been found. The Point Pleasant plate, the only fully intact boundary marker left by the French, remains in the Richmond museum, where it is kept in storage and is viewable by appointment only.

BLOODSHED ON THE OHIO

1774

While Colonel Andrew Lewis of the Virginia Militia had reason to feel safe and secure as he celebrated his fifty-fourth birthday on October 9, 1774, Shawnee Chief Cornstalk was planning an unpleasant surprise party set to begin at dawn the following day.

Lewis, a tall, imposing man with dark brown eyes, spent his birthday at rest, surrounded by a force of eleven hundred well-armed troops under his command. Many of them were friends, neighbors, or relatives, including his thirty-eight-year-old brother, Charles.

As the militiamen listened to Reverend John Terry deliver a birthday sermon honoring their leader, Lewis had time to reflect on the long and arduous journey that had brought him here, to the Kanawha River's confluence with the Ohio, on colonial America's western frontier.

Events set in motion in the spring of 1774 prompted the militiamen's twelve-day, 108-mile march from the Great Levels, a relatively flat, treeless area near the site of present-day Lewisburg, to the unpopulated site where the Elk River flows into the Kanawha, now downtown Charleston. At the mouth of the Elk, Lewis and his men spent a week building eighteen large canoes to carry the bulk of their supplies the remaining sixty miles to the mouth of the Kanawha at what is now Point Pleasant, where they arrived on October 6.

While the land between the Appalachians and the Mississippi had been ceded to Native Americans under the terms of the Proclamation of 1763, settlers had begun clearing land along the Ohio River in the vicinity of Wheeling and had spread downriver to what is now Sistersville by the spring of 1774. At the same time, a large group of settlers led by George Rogers Clark had gathered at the mouth of the Little Kanawha River at present-day Parkersburg in preparation for moving even further down the Ohio to planned settlements in Kentucky.

In retaliation for the encroachment into their territory, Native Americans began robbing and occasionally killing settlers and traders moving down the Ohio. Some settlers, in turn, began to dole out the same treatment to Native Americans they encountered. On April 30, on the west bank of the Ohio a few miles north of Wheeling, a group of settlers ambushed and killed most members of a hunting party that consisted mostly of relatives of Chief Logan, leader of the Mingo people.

In early May, Lord Dunmore, the governor of Virginia, received news of the outbreak of hostilities along the Ohio frontier. He ordered that two large columns of troops—one led by him and the other led by Lewis—converge on Point Pleasant from the north and south to begin a sweeping show of force through the upper Ohio Valley.

Lord Dunmore led the northern column, which marched to Fort Pitt at present-day Pittsburgh and then veered south down the Ohio, while Lewis's column approached from the south, following the Greenbrier and Kanawha rivers. At Point Pleasant, Lewis found a message from Dunmore left in a large hollow tree, instructing him to proceed down the Ohio to the Hocking River in what is now Ohio and then proceed up the Hocking to meet Dunmore at one of a series of Indian villages found along the stream.

Lewis opted to remain at Point Pleasant until his rear guard and remaining supplies arrived from the mouth of the Elk before moving downriver to join the governor's column. But a surprise attack of one thousand Shawnee and Mingo warriors led by Chief Cornstalk on the day following Lewis's birthday prevented the militia colonel from fulfilling his plan.

Cornstalk's raid could have had disastrous consequences for Lewis and his army, had a pair of militia scouts not decided to hunt for deer at daybreak on October 10. It was then that James Mooney and Joseph Hughey encountered an advance element of Cornstalk's force moving through the forest about one mile north of Lewis's camp.

Cornstalk's scouts had followed Lewis's movement down the Kanawha to Point Pleasant. The Shawnee chief had little difficulty assembling an army of Native Americans anxious to drive the soldiers out of the territory they considered theirs. Before dawn on October 10, Cornstalk and his men quietly crossed the Ohio from its western shore, landed on the eastern shore about three miles upstream from the Virginia Militia's encampment, and began stealthily making their way south through the towering hardwoods that lined the river.

Armed with muskets and flintlock rifles as well as tomahawks, Cornstalk's men fired on the militia scouts, who hightailed it back to their camp to sound a warning. Lewis ordered his drummers to beat out a "take arms" signal, and ordered two columns each consisting of 150 men to move toward the approaching Indians. One column of Virginians followed the bank of the Ohio, while the other followed the base of a ridge that parallels the river.

The militiamen encountered Cornstalk's force about three-fourths of a mile upstream of their camp, and came under withering fire. It soon became apparent that they had come up against an army as large, well-armed, and eager to fight as their own.

"Never did Indians stick closer to it, nor behave bolder," wrote Colonel William Fleming, who led one of the columns. Cornstalk's men formed a line across the peninsula leading to Lewis's main force, blocking the route of retreat for the two columns of troops. Over the noise of the firefight, Chief Cornstalk's deep, booming voice could be heard urging on his troops. The Virginians eventually rallied and dispensed a deadly rain of fire of their own in a battle that lasted into the afternoon.

Meanwhile, Lewis ordered three companies of troops to sneak upriver, using a high stretch of riverbank and thick brush for cover, and attack the Indians from the rear. The maneuver proved successful, apparently causing the Indians to believe an army or reinforcements had arrived.

Apparently convinced that he was now outnumbered and outgunned by a superior force, Cornstalk opted to break off the fight, cross the Ohio, and return to friendly villages along the Scioto River in what is now the state of Ohio, allowing the colonials to claim victory.

In a strange twist of fate, among those fighting with the Shawnee in the battle was White Wolf, the former John Ward, who had been kidnapped from his family of Virginia pioneers as a small boy. His father, Captain James Ward, among the militiamen taking part in the engagement, was killed in the battle.

Lewis's force also contained two officers who would later become governors of states to be carved from the frontier to the west. Lieutenant Isaac Shelby served as Kentucky's first governor, while Lieutenant John Sevier was the first governor of Tennessee.

Eighty-one members of Lewis's army were killed or fatally wounded in the bloodiest Indian-settler battle to take place on what is now West Virginia soil. Those killed in action included the commander's brother, Charles Lewis. Cornstalk's warriors carried off most of their dead, but enough bodies remained on the battlefield for the colonial troops to remove eighteen to twenty scalps and retrieve forty guns and eighty blankets.

Not long after smoke cleared from the battlefield at Point Pleasant, Lord Dunmore, camped along the Scioto River south of what is now Columbus, Ohio, negotiated the Treaty of Camp Charlotte with the Shawnee. That short-lived treaty, formalized in Pittsburgh in 1775 by representatives of all the major Ohio tribes, banned white settlement in the Kentucky territory and outlawed hunting by Native Americans south and east of the Ohio River.

Some historians have claimed the Battle of Point Pleasant as the first engagement of America's Revolutionary War, since the British allied with certain Native American tribes during their struggle to crush the colonial rebellion. But the consensus opinion is that Point Pleasant was the most significant engagement of Lord Dunmore's War to safeguard settlement in the Ohio Valley. The battle also made it more difficult for the French and the Spanish, who were moving into the region at the time, to claim land in the Ohio frontier.

Chief Cornstalk's connection to Point Pleasant did not, unfortunately, end on the battlefield in 1774.

In September of 1777, when the British were actively seeking Shawnee support to fight the American rebels, Cornstalk traveled to Fort Randolph, a stockade built by militiamen at Point Pleasant the previous year. Cornstalk, apparently troubled about the prospect of being drawn into a military struggle that would prove costly to his people, came to warn white settlers of British plans.

Suspicious of their former foe, the militiamen detained Cornstalk and his entourage, which included his son, Elinipsico, and his sub-chief, Red Hawk. During their forced stay at the stockade, a settler was killed near the fort. Despite the Indians' obvious lack of involvement in the killing, a revenge-minded mob burst into the room where they were being held and assassinated them.

Shortly after the incident, depositions were taken from Captain John Anderson and two enlisted men who witnessed the incident.

Anderson testified that Captain Matthew Arbuckle, the fort's commander, told "a number of armed men" who entered the garrison "determined to kill the Indians held in custody" to leave, and was in turn told "that it was not in his power" to stop them.

Five settlers were eventually charged with the murders, but no witnesses could be found to testify against them.

STEAMBOAT'S FIRST TEST RUN

1787

On a clear, crisp morning on December 3, 1787, about fifty of the Shepherdstown area's most prominent citizens gathered on a rocky bluff adjacent to a set of sheer, one-hundred-foot cliffs overlooking the town's Potomac River ferry landing.

Among those gathered in the oldest town in what would become the state of West Virginia was General Horatio Gates, whose troops turned the tide of the Revolutionary War in the 1777 victory over the British at the Battle of Saratoga. The immaculately dressed, ruddy-faced Gates owned Traveler's Rest, a plantation located a few miles outside Shepherdstown, which was then a town of about one thousand residents.

Standing next to Gates was burly William Darke, another Shepherdstown area planter and Revolutionary War officer, who would later become a general in the Virginia militia and serve in the Virginia General Assembly.

Moored to the Sherpherdstown shore of the ferry crossing was the object of the crowd's attention—a fifty-foot wooden boat, upon which a metal boiler and network of steam and water pipes took up more than half the deck space. Aboard the craft was James Rumsey, an inventor, gristmill operator, and innkeeper from nearby Bath, who was going through final preparations prior to demonstrating what he and a number of historians would later claim to be the world's first operational steamboat.

As Rumsey pushed his craft off the shore and into the current of the Potomac, he engaged his engine and headed upstream. It was a full twenty years before Robert Fulton powered his *Clermont* up the Hudson River and into the history books as the steamboat's inventor.

While Rumsey and rival Pennsylvania inventor John Fitch, who debuted his first steam-powered vessel a few years later, each designed and built operational steamboats that traveled relatively short distances in the 1780s and 1790s, Fulton's 150-mile voyage of the *Clermont* from New York City to Albany, at an average speed of five miles per hour, was generally considered the first successful demonstration of the steamboat's commercial viability. Rumsey and Fitch still have supporters who insist they should be credited with the development of the steamboat, but Fulton proved that the *Clermont* was more than a curiosity or an experiment, and is generally recognized as the father of the steam-powered watercraft.

Aboard Rumsey's steamboat on that midwinter morning in 1787 were five guests invited to take part in the historic event. Seated behind the boiler were Rumsey's wife, Mary; her sister-in-law, Mrs. Charles Morrow; Morrow's daughter, Ann; and Eleanor Shepherd, wife of Abram Shepherd, warden at Shepherdstown's Classical Academy. At the helm of the boat was Rumsey's brother-in-law, Charles Morrow.

As Morrow steered the prow of the boat to the west, the boat lurched forward, against the current, and to the cheers from the observation knoll, settled into a three-mile-per-hour pace.

General Gates whipped off his hat in excitement, shouting, "My God! She moves!"

The boat traveled upstream about a half mile, returned past the ferry landing, and moved downstream and out of town for a short distance before repeating the loop. By then, hundreds of onlookers had flocked to the side of the Potomac to watch. After two hours of travel under steam, Rumsey returned to the launch site to a chorus of cheers and shouts of congratulations.

There were no paddlewheels attached to Rumsey's watercraft. Instead, he used a propulsion system similar to that used by today's jet boats and personal watercraft. Rumsey connected a hydraulic pump piston directly to the piston of a Newcomen steam engine. The pump took in water from near the keel and, using a flexible diaphragm, ejected it at the stern, enabling forward motion.

Rumsey's keen inventive mind attracted the attention of George Washington, a frequent visitor to the town of Bath (later known as Berkeley Springs), where Rumsey was a partner in an inn, the Sign of the Liberty Pole and Flag, with a distant relative of Washington.

After the Revolutionary War, Washington, who bought two lots in Bath in 1776, hired Rumsey to build a vacation home and stable on the property. Rumsey was also commissioned to build the first public bathhouses at Berkeley Springs. In 1785, Washington appointed Rumsey superintendent of the Potomac Improvement Company, an organization formed to make the Potomac River navigable from Georgetown in present-day Washington, DC, to the mouth of the Shenandoah River at Harpers Ferry. The company Rumsey briefly managed was the precursor of the Chesapeake & Potomac Canal Co.

Constantly plagued by financial woes, Rumsey left the Shepherdstown area in 1788 and moved to Philadelphia to seek funding for building bigger and better steamboats. There, Benjamin

Franklin helped Rumsey form the Rumseyan Society, a group that bankrolled an extended trip to England where Rumsey hoped to raise the cash needed to commercially produce his steamboat.

Rumsey ended up spending four years in England. On December 20, 1792, just after delivering a lecture to the Society of Mechanical Arts and the day before he was to demonstrate his newest steamboat, the one-hundred-foot *Columbia Maid*, he died after suffering a severe headache.

The man Thomas Jefferson described as "the most original and greatest mechanical genius I have ever seen" was buried in London, and his work was overshadowed by Fulton's 1807 demonstration of a commercially successful steamboat.

Today, the most enduring tribute to the self-taught inventor is the Rumsey Monument, a seventy-five-foot-tall granite column topped by a globe, which towers above the knoll from which spectators watched Rumsey's two-hour steamboat demonstration in 1787.

THOMAS JEFFERSON'S LION

1796

In 1796, workers digging saltpeter in a limestone cave owned by Frederick Gromer in the Second Creek Valley of present-day Monroe County uncovered a huge thighbone from an unknown creature. After speculating briefly over the origin of the femur, the workers quickly put it to practical use. They split one end of the bone and used it as a brace to support the side of a vat used in processing saltpeter into the primary component of gunpowder.

In the days that followed, more strange bones emerged from the saltpeter accumulation in Haynes Cave, as the cavern was later known. Word of the discoveries soon reached the ears of Colonel John Stuart, a Revolutionary War officer who had become the largest landowner in this newly settled section of the Trans-Allegheny Frontier.

Colonel Stuart, who lived just a few miles from the cave, was a long-time acquaintance of, and correspondent with, Thomas Jefferson, who had justly earned a reputation as a man of science in addition to being a successful planter, skilled statesman, and vice president of the United States when Stuart contacted him about the mysterious bones.

Jefferson received from Colonel Stuart another femur from the unknown creature, along with an ulna or forearm bone, six bones from the animal's feet, and three claws, the longest of which measured nearly eight inches. He soon concluded that the bones belonged to a large quadruped.

"I will venture to refer to him by the name of Great Claw, or Megalonyx, to which he seems sufficiently entitled by the distinguished size of that member," he said in issuing a report on the discovery of the bones during a 1797 meeting of the American Philosophical Society in Philadelphia.

Jefferson consulted with French naturalist Louis Jean-Marie Daubenton to compute an estimated size for the creature. Using Daubenton's formula for estimating the size of lions from the dimensions of their bones, he estimated that his Great Claw was a little over five feet long and weighed about 260 pounds.

Taking into account the animal's huge claws and skeletal remains indicating it was a lion-sized quadruped, Jefferson speculated at the Philadelphia conference that Megalonyx was some type of large cat. He told scientists at the meeting that ancient Native American petroglyphs found on a rock at the mouth of the Kanawha River near present-day Point Pleasant depicted "a perfect figure of a lion" that may have roamed the region long before settlers arrived. He also theorized that Great Claw flourished during the age of a long-ago climate shift, possibly caused by a comet impacting with Earth, creating an era "when our latitudes suited the lion and other animals of that temperament."

The scientific discussion of his findings, along with the presentation of a paper on the topic and the donation of the West Virginia bones, led to Jefferson being credited for initiating the science of vertebrate paleontology in the United States.

Two years after Jefferson made his Philadelphia appearance, Dr. Caspar Wistar correctly identified the Haynes Cave bones as belonging to a type of giant ground sloth. The species was named *Megalonyx jeffersonii,* or Jefferson's giant ground sloth, in 1822.

Jefferson, not completely certain that the species was extinct, urged Meriwether Lewis to be alert for any signs of the creature when he and William Clark explored the untrammeled land of the Louisiana Purchase from 1804 to 1806.

Subsequent research indicates that *Megalonyx jeffersonii* roamed the continent between 10,000 and 150,000 years ago, from West Virginia to Alaska. The animals grew to be up to ten feet in length, weighed up to eight hundred pounds, and could stand on their hind legs to feed on tree leaves.

In 2008, the West Virginia Legislature designated *Megalonyx jeffersonii* the state's official fossil. The bones from Haynes Cave are now in the collection of the Academy of Natural Sciences in Philadelphia.

Now managed by the West Virginia Cave Conservancy, Haynes Cave is better known these days for its surviving saltpeter manufacturing remnants, including hoppers, plank bridges, and a rope and windlass system dating back to the late 1700s and early 1800s.

CONSPIRACY ISLAND

1805

By May of 1805, Harman and Margaret Blennerhassett had entertained their share of prominent visitors to the Ohio frontier at their idyllic island estate in the middle of the Ohio River, two miles downstream from Parkersburg.

But hosting a dinner for Aaron Burr, a former vice president of the United States and a man very much in the news at the time, was an experience to be savored. Conversation continued long after their servants cleared the last of the imported china and silverware from the table in the dining room of their huge Palladian mansion, and ended only when the midnight hour drew near.

Burr landed on the Blennerhassetts' narrow, three-mile-long island the week after departing from Pittsburgh on April 29 for a series of meetings in far-flung cities along the Ohio and Mississippi Rivers. The young couple's oasis of wealth and gentility on a frontier rife with rude cabins and hand-to-mouth living would have been difficult to pass by, especially for Burr, who was looking for backers to support his new off-the-books empire-building scheme.

Burr's involvement in conventional politics had come to a screeching halt the year before he encountered the Blennerhassetts. In 1804, after stepping down as vice president at the end of Thomas Jefferson's first term, Burr lost a bid to become governor of New York, thanks in part to the efforts of political rival Alexander Hamilton. On July 11, 1804, Burr challenged Hamilton to a duel, during which he fatally wounded the founding father. With warrants for his arrest pending in his home state of New York and New Jersey, where the duel took place, Burr, his zeal for shaping history unabated, turned his attention to the west.

In recent months, Burr had been in contact with British diplomats to gauge whether their government would support a scheme to carve a new nation from a section of the vast Louisiana Purchase lands recently purchased from Spain. Burr was also interested in raising funds to bankroll a private military expedition to seize a section of Mexico, then a Spanish territory, and make it an independent nation to be ruled by him.

The Blennerhassetts were just the type of people Burr was hoping to meet—wealthy, ambitious freethinkers who were willing to take risks and spend money.

Harman Blennerhassett, the son of Irish aristocrats, attended Trinity College in Dublin and later studied law at the Inns of Court in London. Margaret, his dark-haired, blue-eyed wife, was conversant in French and Italian and was a scholar of literature. The couple left Ireland in 1796 shortly after Harman sold the family estate he inherited, moving to America in part to escape the scandal caused by the fact that Margaret was Harman's niece as well as his wife.

In 1798, while taking a flatboat journey down the Ohio River to find an Eden-like locale in which to build a new life in the New World, the Blennerhassetts glided past a densely wooded uninhabited island near the mouth of the Little Kanawha River. They bought half the island and lived in a log blockhouse while their eight-thousand-square-foot mansion was being built. Completed in 1800, the mansion was filled with books, musical instruments, and imported furnishings, and was surrounded by nine acres of landscaped gardens and lawns.

There is no doubt that during his brief time spent with the couple on their island, Burr shared some of the details of his newest scheme to acquire land and power in the southwest. Seven months after Burr's visit, Harman Blennerhassett wrote a letter to the former vice president:

"I should be honored in being associated with you, in any contemplated enterprise you would permit me to participate in. . . . Viewing the probability of a rupture with Spain, I am disposed, in the confidential spirit of this letter, to offer you my friends' and my own services in any contemplated measures in which you may embark."

Burr took the Irishman up on his offer. By the summer of 1806, Blennerhassett Island had become a staging area for Burr's venture. Blennerhassett was overseeing the construction of fifteen boats capable of carrying five hundred men, and placing orders for large amounts of flour, pork, cornmeal, whiskey, and other supplies.

Blennerhassett told some of the recruits arriving at the island that war with Spain was imminent and that Mexico was the ultimate destination of the small armada being assembled.

In late August of 1806, Burr returned to the Ohio River island with nearly fifty men who were to form the core of his expeditionary force. In a coded letter, Burr wrote that his remaining forces would rendezvous on the Ohio in November, and then travel down the Mississippi River to Natchez by early December to merge with a force he thought was being raised by General James Wilkinson, the US Army's ranking general and one of Burr's oldest friends.

But unknown to Burr, Wilkinson—the man to whom he had sent the coded letter—had dropped out of the plot, forwarded Burr's letter to President Jefferson, and ordered troops along the Mississippi to be on the alert for Burr's arrival.

Meanwhile, militia officials in Virginia and Ohio were made aware of Blennerhassett's role in Burr's venture. On December 7, 1806, four boats and thirty of Burr's men arrived on the island, but two days later, militiamen raided a boatyard in nearby Marietta, Ohio, and seized the remaining eleven boats Blennerhassett had arranged to have built. On the night of December 9, after hearing about the seizure, Blennerhassett and his thirty men headed downstream under the cover of darkness, avoiding a raid on Blennerhassett Island the following day, during which the mansion was heavily damaged.

Both Burr and Blennerhassett were captured near Natchez in early 1807. Later that year they stood trial on charges of treason. While the government established that Burr raised money and assembled men and supplies on Blennerhassett Island, it could not prove that the two committed overt actions of treason, as required by law. Both men were released from custody.

Blennerhassett sold his island estate shortly after the trial and briefly practiced law in Canada. The mansion burned to the ground in 1811. Blennerhassett died in relative poverty on Guernsey Island in the English Channel in 1822.

Blennerhassett Island is now a West Virginia State Park. A replica of the mansion has been painstakingly built on the site of the original Blennerhassett home.

WHITEWATER JUSTICE

1812

On a late September morning in 1812, John Marshall, the fifty-seven-year-old chief justice of the US Supreme Court, arose from his bedroll at a campsite on a rocky island in the mouth of the Greenbrier River, stretched his lanky frame, and turned his dark brown eyes toward the gorge that lay downstream.

At Marshall's campsite, now a part of the present-day town of Hinton, the Greenbrier River flows into the larger New River, which tumbles northward for seventy miles over scores of rapids, some of them equal to the most challenging in the world, as it makes its way to its confluence with the Gauley River.

Between expanses of sheer sandstone cliffs, the canyon walls that towered nearly one thousand feet above the cascading river were covered with chestnut, oak, and other hardwood trees still in their summer greenery when Marshall first laid eyes on them.

At that time, the birth of West Virginia's whitewater rafting industry, which annually enables tens of thousands of thrill seekers to run the New River Gorge's mightiest rapids, was 150 years in the future. When Marshall arrived at Hinton, no white explorer or surveyor had traveled the length of the gorge by boat, and few had traversed the narrow, boulder-strewn, rhododendron-choked floor of the canyon on foot or on horseback.

Instead of the lightweight, highly maneuverable self-bailing inflatable rafts used by today's New River runners, Marshall and his crew of four or five boatmen on this day would launch their bid to travel the turbulent gorge in a leaky, ungainly, sixty-foot-long, seven-foot-wide wooden bateaux.

Bateaux were commonly used to carry supplies on the relatively placid waters of the James River between the Virginia cities of Richmond and Covington. Marshall, in addition to being the chief justice of the US Supreme Court, was an officer and major stockholder in the James River & Kanawha Company. In 1812, the Virginia General Assembly authorized the company to conduct a survey to determine the feasibility of developing a trans-Allegheny water route between the James River at Covington and the Kanawha River, which begins at the end of the gorge where the New merges with the Gauley.

Bateaux traffic was already occurring on the Kanawha, linking the Charleston area, where salt was a key export, to the easily navigable Ohio River at Point Pleasant, at the time of Marshall's voyage. If salt and other raw materials produced west of the Alleghenies could be boated eastward to Richmond and traded for manufactured goods, the young nation's commercial possibilities could be dramatically boosted.

On September 29, 1812, Marshall and his crew, which included fellow James River & Kanawha Company commissioner Andrew Alexander, pushed away from the shore of their Greenbrier River island and used a stern-mounted sweeping oar/rudder to steer their way around the boulders that dotted their first stretch of the New River.

While the trip ahead of them was potentially life threatening, the journey that brought them to this point had been no picnic.

After poling their way up the James without incident to Covington, Marshall and his crew loaded their bateaux on a wagon and rolled it through a gap in the Alleghenies to a launch site on the Greenbrier River between Lewisburg and White Sulphur Springs.

While huge standing waves, plunging waterfalls and mile-long chains of rapids would pose challenges on the New River, it was a lack of water that made the survey party's Greenbrier River leg such an ordeal.

"The labor of removing stones, and of dragging the boat over those which could not be moved, was so great that your Commissioners at one time were enabled to advance only three miles in two days, even with the assistance of a horse and of many additional laborers," Marshall wrote.

In all, it took ten days to make the trip from the Lewisburg area to the New River at Hinton—a trip that in June, when the Greenbrier is usually running much higher, "might have been performed in a single day," according to Marshall.

Once afloat on the New River, Marshall, a former Revolutionary War captain who had endured the winter of 1777 at Valley Forge, quickly learned that he was in for an ordeal of a different nature. The New, he discovered, "exhibits an almost continued succession of shoals and falls, from which the navigator is sometimes, though rarely, relieved by a fine sheet of deep placid water."

The lower end of the gorge, Marshall recounted, offered his bateaux crew a "scene awful and discouraging. . . . In some places, for a mile or more in continuation, it is compressed by the mountains on each side into a channel narrowed by enormous rocks which lie promiscuously in the bed of the river, through which it is often difficult to find a passage wide enough for the admission of a boat."

Marshall's crew used ropes and wooden skids to lower their huge boat, which weighed between two thousand and three thousand pounds, through Sandstone Falls to avoid a twenty-three-foot plunge off a sandstone ledge. They used ropes to walk the unloaded boat through other life-threatening cataracts from the shoreline.

When the battered, leaking plank boat reached the mouth of the Gauley River at present-day Gauley Bridge, Marshall and his weary men became the first in recorded history to navigate the New River Gorge.

Marshall credited the skills of his crew with the successful first descent.

"This voyage was performed by boatmen who, having never before seen the river, were reduced to the necessity of selecting their way at the moment, without the aid of previous information," he wrote.

Marshall, a former Revolutionary War captain, recommended making the New River Gorge suitable for navigation by building locks around the larger waterfalls and blasting channels through the most difficult whitewater sections. He also suggested cutting a towpath along one side of the river on which horses could pull upstream-bound boats.

Due to the extreme expense that would have been involved in fulfilling Marshall's vision for the remote, rugged gorge, none of his recommendations came into being, and no one else was known to have navigated the gorge until 1869, when railroad tycoon Collis P. Huntington and two boatmen made the trip in another wooden boat to survey a possible rail line through the canyon.

Unlike Marshall's voyage, Huntington's trip bore industrial fruit. A rail line was completed through the gorge in the early 1870s. Bateaux were initially used to supply construction crews, but use of the wooden boats was soon abandoned due to numerous incidents of sinking and drowning.

Marshall's imprint on West Virginia endured in other ways.

His narrow Constitutional interpretation of treason laws five years before the New River voyage made possible the acquittal of frontier aristocrat Harman Blennerhassett of Wood County and former Vice President Aaron Burr for plotting to carve out an empire in the southwest.

West Virginia's second largest institution of higher learning, Marshall University, is named in honor of the chief justice for his efforts to increase voting rights and representation for western Virginians during the Virginia Constitutional Convention of 1829–1830.

For years, the sheer cliff overlooking the New River at Hawks Nest State Park's main overlook was known as Marshall's Pillars. But there was to be no justice in honoring the chief justice for his role as a whitewater pioneer. Today, roadside markers identify the pillar-like cliff as Lover's Leap.

WORLD'S LONGEST
SUSPENSION BRIDGE

1849

Supported by timbers anchored to twelve steel cables stretched ninety feet above the surface of the Ohio River, crews of workmen secured deck planks to the world's longest suspension bridge with three-fourths-inch wire stays, steadily making their way toward the midpoint of the stream from the Ohio and Virginia shores.

Though it was barely mid-morning, more than one thousand people had gathered along the banks of the Ohio on October 19, 1849, to witness the historic completion of the Wheeling Suspension Bridge, an engineering marvel that would hasten America's westward expansion and enhance Wheeling's role as a major supply depot for westbound settlers.

The National Road, America's first federally funded highway, had connected Wheeling to Baltimore via Cumberland, Maryland, for the past thirty years. The road, which would later become US 40, extended westward to Vandalia, Illinois, leaving traffic bottlenecked at Wheeling, where wagon drovers relied on a time-consuming ferry service to cross the main channel of the Ohio.

Completion of any bridge was cause enough for celebration, but having that bridge take shape as a towering, graceful structure with the world's longest suspension span was icing on the cake and a huge source of regional pride.

By 10 a.m., someone had placed the Stars and Stripes atop the highest stone support tower on the Wheeling side of the bridge, and a short time later, the Ohio state flag appeared on the span's westernmost tower—even though it was on Zane's Island, claimed by Virginia. A covered bridge completed thirteen years earlier across the back channel of the Ohio River connected the western shore of Zane's Island to Ohio soil.

The official dedication ceremony for the record-breaking 1,010-foot-long span was one month distant, but a spontaneous public celebration was in the works. Before the last echoes of hammers being used to nudge the planks into position faded from the hills surrounding the river, bridge engineer Charles Ellet, a dark-haired, French-educated Pennsylvanian, and I. Dickinson, his superintendent of iron and stonework, drove a one-horse carriage onto the new decking from the Wheeling side of the structure.

"The carriage proceeded onward amid the breathless anxiety of the assembled multitude who watched it rolling like a triumphal chariot at its dizzy height, through the air," the *Daily Wheeling Gazette* reported. "The roar of cannon soon announced its safe arrival at the western shore, and a long, loud, and triumphant shout broke from the thousands of delighted spectators."

A few hours after Ellet and Dickinson made the first crossing on the new bridge, a tiny carriage pulled by a team of Shetland ponies rolled across the span, in an apparent publicity stunt engineered by promoter P. T. Barnum. The carriage was used by Barnum's star little person, General Tom Thumb, in an 1844 tour of England, during which the twenty-nine-inch-tall Thumb had an audience with Queen Victoria. While Thumb did not arrive in town in time to make the crossing in the carriage, "his footmen and aide-de-camps were there, and proceeded with the most admirable grace and dignity," the Wheeling newspaper reported.

Five days after General Tom Thumb's carriage traversed the bridge, a six-horse team pulling a heavily laden National Road freight wagon made the crossing, accounting for the first commercial use of the span. Ellet calculated that his bridge could easily accommodate thirty-two similar six-horse wagonloads, plus five hundred pedestrians, at a time.

When the bridge was officially dedicated on November 15, 1849, Congressman R. W. Thompson of Indiana, who fought for federal funding for the bridge, said that the idea of completing such an engineering feat had been "laughed at with derision only a few years ago, and even now staggers the imagination of the world—the bridging of one of our great rivers by a single span of 1,010 feet. I feel with you a just pride for the sake of our common country in commemorating this extraordinary achievement of American ingenuity and skill."

Men and women spent the afternoon strolling their way across the span, greeting friends from both sides of the river, as bands played and cannons fired salutes. At dusk, one thousand gas lamps were illuminated and artfully arranged across the bridge railings, cables, and piers, creating "an elegant and graceful curve of fire high above the river that was never excelled in beauty," according to a newspaper account of the ceremony.

The Wheeling Suspension Bridge retained its "world's longest" title for only two years, when the Queenston-Lewiston Bridge across the Niagara River at Lewiston, New York, was completed. That span was thirty feet longer than the Wheeling Bridge.

Civic leaders in Pittsburgh, who saw their city's status as a major embarkation point for western commerce eroded by Wheeling's new bridge, filed suit to have it removed, ostensibly because it interfered with upriver steamboat navigation on the Ohio. They claimed that the bridge deck would clip off the smokestacks of riverboats traveling to and from Pittsburgh by way of Wheeling. After attorneys representing Wheeling established that the bridge provided adequate clearance for all steamboats except during extreme high water events, when navigation was unlikely anyway, a few Pittsburgh-based boat owners raised their smokestacks from the sixty-foot norm to eighty feet.

Wheeling eventually prevailed in the legal wrangling, but Mother Nature ended up accomplishing what Pittsburgh's lawyers could not on May 17, 1854, when a violent gale overturned the bridge deck and left it in twisted ruins in the river below. It took nearly two years to reopen the bridge, using a narrower deck made mainly from materials recycled from the storm wreckage. In 1872, the bridge was restored to its original width and symmetry.

While the original Wheeling Suspension Bridge was built over two years at a cost of about $135,000, the West Virginia Department of Highways spent $2.4 million in 1982 to restore its cables and anchorages and rebuild its trusses.

The Wheeling span is the first bridge to be designated a National Historic Monument.

Today, it provides the only access to Zane's Island, now known as Wheeling Island, site of a tree-lined residential neighborhood of historic homes, as well as a popular race track and casino complex.

The bridge Ellert and Dickinson first rolled across in their one-horse carriage in 1849 is now the world's oldest vehicular suspension bridge still in use.

JOHN BROWN'S FIRST CASUALTY

1859

While the night of October 16, 1859, marked the beginning of abolitionist John Brown's raid on the federal arsenal at Harpers Ferry, for Heyward Shepherd, a free black baggage handler and substitute clerk at the town's Baltimore & Ohio Railroad station, it was just another day at work.

Like many others in Harpers Ferry that night, Shepherd was unaware that Brown and an army of twenty-one abolitionists had crossed the Potomac from a nearby training camp on Maryland's side of the river, and were implementing a plan to seize the US Arsenal. Brown and his followers believed that by seizing the munitions depot, located a short walk from the B & O station, and taking control of its huge stockpile of weapons, enslaved blacks in the region would be encouraged to rise up and join them. Then, armed and motivated, they would sweep through the south to free other slaves.

By midnight, Brown and his followers had cut telegraph lines entering the town, captured a train, and detained several night watchmen and guards. Shortly after 1:30 a.m. on October 17, just after the express train from Wheeling arrived at the Harpers Ferry station, Shepherd walked to the nearby railroad bridge crossing the Potomac. There he was confronted by two of Brown's armed men, who ordered him to halt. Instead, Shepherd turned and ran toward the station and was shot in the back. Several agonizing hours later, the African-American railroad worker became the first of sixteen people to die in a raid designed to end black oppression.

In the hours before dawn, Brown and his followers captured the federal arsenal and seized a number of townspeople as hostages. When workers arrived at the arsenal the following morning and found it in control of Brown and his raiders, they and local militia members surrounded the brick building and began firing on its occupants. Brown and his men took nine hostages, barricaded themselves in the arsenal's engine house, and traded gunfire with militiamen and townspeople.

In Washington, DC, about sixty miles to the east, President Patrick Buchanan was made aware of the raid. At mid-afternoon, he ordered a detachment of US Marines to proceed at haste to Harpers Ferry. Placed in command of the Marine squad was US Army Colonel Robert E. Lee, who, less than three years later, would command the army of the Confederate States of America.

Lee sent his aide, Lieutenant J.E.B. Stuart, who would also later become a renowned Confederate general, to negotiate a surrender agreement with Brown. After Brown refused to surrender, the Marines stormed the building, capturing Brown and his surviving followers in a matter of minutes.

While the raid ended quickly, its consequences were far reaching.

Within a matter of weeks, at the Jefferson County Courthouse in Charles Town, Brown was tried and found guilty of treason against the Commonwealth of Virginia, of which Harpers Ferry was then a part. He was hanged in Charles Town on December 2. Among spectators watching his execution was actor John Wilkes Booth, who would later assassinate President Abraham Lincoln.

Brown instantly became a martyr for abolitionists across the nation, and his name was linked with pro-Union, anti-slavery beliefs, accelerating America's march toward the Civil War.

While Brown's death had immediate and far-reaching implications, comparatively little was written or said about Shepherd's death until long after the Civil War had ended, when he became an icon of proponents of the "faithful slave" philosophy.

While it seems more likely that Shepherd died because he feared for his life and ran when two white strangers attempted to detain him at gunpoint in the middle of the night, the B&O worker was portrayed in some press accounts as a man whose life was cut short because he rejected abolitionism and refused to disrupt the existing social system.

In the early 1900s, organizations like the United Daughters of the Confederacy and the Sons of Confederate Veterans began paying tribute not only to fallen southern soldiers, but also to the slaves and servants who did not rebel against their masters during the Civil War. Despite the fact that Shepherd was not a slave, and that there was no clear picture of his philosophical inclinations at the time of the raid, he became the United Daughters of the Confederacy's prime candidate for a proposed "Faithful Slave Monument."

During the UDC annual convention in 1920, president-general Mary McKinney told members that Shepherd was killed "because he held too dear the lives of 'Ole Massa' and 'ole Miss'us,' to fulfill Brown's orders of rapine and murder. The hero of Harpers Ferry was not Brown, a soldier of fortune, but a black man who gave his life for his friends."

The UDC delegates voted to join the Sons of Confederate Veterans in building a monument in Harpers Ferry "to the faithful slave who gave his life in defense of his master during the John Brown raid."

By the time the monument was eventually unveiled on October 10, 1931, Shepherd's status had been amended from contented slave to "industrious and respected colored freeman" and railroad employee who "became the first victim of the attempted insurrection" by John Brown.

But the wording on the monument went on to assert that Shepherd exemplified "the character and faithfulness of thousands of Negroes who, throughout many temptations through subsequent years of war, so conducted themselves that no stain was left upon a record which is the peculiar heritage of the American people, and an everlasting tribute to the best in both races."

About four hundred people attended the dedication ceremony for the granite boulder marker at the corner of Potomac and Shenandoah streets. There, Matthew P. Andrews of the Sons of Confederate Veterans described Brown as a crazed man consumed by "some kind of warped psychosis," and said slavery in the United States was "preferable to the bondage of both soul and body which enveloped the life of the majority of those captured on the Congo." Elizabeth Bashinski, president-general of the UDC at the time, told the crowd that the monument "commemorates the loyalty, courage and self-sacrifice of Heyward Shepherd and thousands of his race who would, like him, have suffered death rather than betray their masters."

A choral group from Storer College, founded in Harpers Ferry immediately after the Civil War to train African-American teachers, was scheduled to perform after the speeches by Andrews and Bashinsky. But before they did, choir director Pearl Tatum gave an impromptu speech of her own:

*I am the daughter of a Connecticut volunteer, who
wore the blue, who fought for the freedom of my people,
for which John Brown struck the first blow.*

*Today we are looking forward to the future, forget-
ting those things of the past. We are pushing forward to
a larger freedom, not in the spirit of the black mammy
but in the spirit of new freedom and rising youth.*

Internationally known author and civil rights activist W.E.B.
DuBois, upon hearing of the ceremony, termed it a "pro-slavery
celebration."

Controversy over the monument continued long after its
dedication ceremony. In 1976, after the National Park Service
bought the land on which the monument stood as part of Harpers
Ferry National Historic Park, the monument was removed to the
park's maintenance yard to protect it from construction activities.
In 1980, members of the SCV and UDC complained that the
monument should be removed from storage and again placed at its
original site. In 1981, the monument was returned to the original
site, but was later covered with a plywood crate when reports were
received of plans to deface it.

In 1995, following complaints by US Senator Jesse Helms,
R-SC, and officials from the SCV and UDC, the plywood cover
was removed from the monument. But next to it, a new interpretive
panel appeared to create a context for the marker:

*On October 17, 1859, abolitionist John Brown
attacked Harpers Ferry to launch a war against slavery.
Heyward Shepherd, a free African-American railroad
baggage master, was shot and killed by Brown's men
shortly after midnight.*

Seventy-two years later, on October 10, 1931, a crowd estimated to include three hundred whites and one hundred blacks gathered to unveil and dedicate the Shepherd Monument.

During the ceremony, voices rose to praise and denounce the monument. Conceived around the turn of the century, the monument endured controversy. In 1905, the United Daughters of the Confederacy stated that "erecting the monument would influence for good the present and coming generations, and prove that the people of the South who owned slaves valued and respected their good qualities as no one else ever did or will do.

After the monument was unveiled in 1995, James Tolbert, the president of the West Virginia chapter of the National Association for the Advancement of Colored People, said the monument "is a misrepresentation of the life and role of Heyward Shepherd. . . . I don't think it's history."

Ideally, Tolbert said, the monument "should be taken by crane to the Potomac River and dropped at the river's deepest point."

PHILIPPI MOM FIRES SHOT HEARD 'ROUND THE WORLD

1861

Sounds made by hundreds of boots slogging down the muddy road fronting her home on the outskirts of Philippi awakened Matilda Humphreys in the dim light of a rainy dawn on June 3, 1861.

When Mrs. Humphreys got up and peered into the sodden gloom to investigate the source of the commotion, she was startled to discover a column of Union soldiers marching into town.

In the opening weeks of the Civil War, Philippi was a hotbed of secessionist sympathizers, and Mrs. Humphreys counted herself among them. In downtown Philippi, the seat of government in Barbour County, a palmetto tree flag had flown over the county courthouse since February, showing the town's support for South Carolina, the first state to secede from the Union.

Two weeks before the arrival of the Union troops, one of Mrs. Humphreys' sons, Lorenzo, had enlisted in the Barbour Grays, a locally raised Confederate infantry company. Lorenzo Humphreys was one of about 750 fresh, barely trained Confederate soldiers camped in Philippi when the federal force marched past his mother's home. Fearing that the Union force would take Lorenzo and his comrades by surprise, Mrs. Humphreys awakened her twelve-year-old son, Oliver, and instructed him to ride into town and alert his brother.

Oliver managed to enter a barn and mount a horse without being detected, but as he reined the steed onto the road, federal troops under the command of Colonel Ebenezer Dumont wrestled him off his mount and onto the ground, as his mother watched in dismay. She fired a shot from a pistol in the direction of the soldiers subduing her son, striking no one. But the gunshot, if not heard 'round the world, reverberated across the soon to be war-torn nation: It set in motion the first land battle of the Civil War.

Unknown to Mrs. Humphreys, a second column of Union soldiers had marched overnight over a series of back roads from a rail siding at Thornton, about twelve miles distant, and was approaching the back end of Philippi. Hours behind schedule due to heavy rains and difficulty following the little-used roads at night, that force, led by Colonel Benjamin Franklin Kelley, was to have fired a single gunshot to signal Dumont that it had arrived in position and that a two-pronged assault on Philippi was to begin.

On June 2, when the siege of Philippi was being planned, Dumont and Kelley expected both forces—each containing about fifteen hundred men—to arrive in position in time for a 4 a.m. attack on the unsuspecting Confederates. But on June 3, 4 a.m. passed with no signal shot being heard. When dawn began to break over the sleepy town, there was still no indication that Kelley's column had arrived.

Anxious to be ready to attack the instant Kelley's force was in position, Colonel Frederick Lander, Dumont's aide de camp, ordered members of the 1st Ohio Light Artillery to bring two cannons and follow him to the summit of Talbott Hill. From there,

Lander and the artillerymen had an unobstructed view of downtown Philippi and the town's landmark three-hundred-foot-long covered bridge over the Tygart Valley River. Out of view inside the bridge, dozens of Rebel soldiers were sleeping, protected from rainfall, while the rest of their comrades dozed in tents and stables.

Soon, Lander and the artillerymen watched in alarm as some of the enemy troops began to stir. Then the sound of the Matilda Humphrey's pistol shot broke the early morning silence. Lander may have thought the shot came from Kelley's overdue column, or he may have simply concluded that whatever its source, it provided ample reason to launch the attack immediately to maintain an element of surprise over the Confederates.

Lander ordered the artillery battery to commence firing, and watched its first volley strike near a small collection of Confederate tents. At last, he could also see the vanguard of Kelley's force approaching the outskirts of Philippi from the east.

Lander, an explorer and surveyor in the American west before the war, rode his horse down the wooded face of Talbott Hill at breakneck pace and thundered across the covered bridge to coordinate a blocking maneuver with Kelley, as Dumont's column marched into town from the west.

Kelley, hearing gunshots and cannon fire, also galloped into town from the east, shooting at fleeing Confederate troops as he went. The rebel troops returned fire, with one of them striking Kelley in the chest. The wound was initially believed to be fatal, but Kelley later recovered, was promoted to brigadier general, and returned to the war.

As the federal troops stormed into town and the small hilltop artillery battery continued to send six-pound balls of solid shot raining down on the Confederates, the southern troops fled town, leaving most of their armaments and supplies behind. Their commander, Colonel George Porterfield, managed to regroup most of his troops at the southeastern edge of the town and make an orderly retreat to Beverly, along the Fairmont-Beverly Turnpike.

While Union troops had spent the night marching through the rain and mud to launch their surprise attack, the battle was over within thirty minutes, giving the engagement the nickname the "Philippi Races." The federal soldiers were too tired and hungry to give chase to the Confederates.

Although no one was killed in the battle, four Union soldiers were wounded, and twenty-six Confederate troops were captured or wounded.

In addition to being the first land battle of the Civil War, the engagement at Philippi produced a number of other "firsts," including the world's first use of the railroad to deploy multiple forces in attacking an enemy objective. Dumont and his men traveled from Grafton to Webster by rail before marching on to Philippi, while Kelley's column rode in railcars from Grafton to Thornton to begin their overland trek to the battle site.

The battle also produced the first of what would become nearly fifty thousand amputees by war's end.

James E. Hanger, eighteen, of Churchville, Virginia, arrived in Philippi the day before the battle, traveling with a wagon train bringing supplies to members of the Churchville Cavalry, which included two of his brothers. Hanger, an engineering student at Washington College in Lexington, Virginia, enlisted in his hometown's unit shortly after arriving, and spent his first night as a soldier sleeping in a stable to avoid the soaking rain.

While the 1st Ohio Light Artillery managed to fire only twelve rounds before the Battle of Philippi ended, one of them bounced off a support beam in Hanger's temporary quarters and struck the unlucky enlistee's left leg, shattering his thigh. Union soldiers found the Virginia youth bleeding in a hayloft and carried him to the Philippi's Methodist Episcopal Church, where James Robison, a surgeon assigned to an Ohio infantry regiment, removed the remnants of his leg seven inches below the hip. No anesthesia was available for the procedure.

Hanger was allowed to recuperate for several days at a field hospital at a Philippi area farm and then was transferred to Camp Chase, a prisoner of war facility in Columbus, Ohio. In August of 1861, he was exchanged for a Union prisoner of war and sent home to Virginia.

"I cannot look back on those days in the hospital without a shudder," Hanger later recalled. "No one can know what such a loss means unless he has suffered a similar catastrophe. In a twinkling of an eye, life's fondest hopes seemed dead. I was in the prey of despair. What could the world hold for a maimed, crippled man?"

Quite a lot, as it turned out.

Hanger locked himself in his upstairs bedroom from August to November of 1861. When he finally emerged, he was walking on a new, hinged artificial leg he had fabricated from hand-whittled barrel staves.

Hanger had developed the world's first articulating prosthetic knee joint, and by the end of 1861 the Virginia legislature had commissioned him to manufacture the "Hanger Limb" for other wounded Confederate veterans. After the war, he patented his artificial leg and sold it across the world.

"Today I am thankful for what seemed then to me nothing but a blunder of fate, but which was to prove instead a great opportunity," Hanger said at the height of his career.

Today, Hanger Orthopedic Group is an eight-hundred-million-dollar business, operating more than six hundred patient care centers worldwide.

Matilda Humphreys sent three of her sons marching off to fight with the Confederate army during the remaining years of the Civil War. One of them, Richard, was killed three years after hostilities broke out in his hometown, when Union forces commanded by General Ulysses S. Grant overwhelmed his Virginia regiment during the Battle of Spotsylvania Courthouse.

STATEHOOD STICKUP

1861

While most successful bank robberies involve an element of stealth and surprise, the June 30, 1861, holdup of the Exchange Bank of Virginia in the Lewis County town of Weston was a glaring exception.

At 5 a.m. on that date, many of the town's 820 residents were awakened by the sound of fifes, drums, and hundreds of marching boots as members of the 7th Ohio Infantry entered the sleeping community and set up a perimeter adjacent to the construction site of a new state mental hospital.

With that task completed, Colonel Erastus Tyler, the regiment's bearded, balding commander, ordered Captain John List and a squad of armed troops to march back into downtown Weston and seize, by use of force if necessary, thirty thousand dollars in gold coins from the bank.

The Trans-Allegheny Lunatic Asylum, authorized by the Virginia General Assembly in 1858, was in its early phase of construction, with only one wing partially complete when the 7th Ohio arrived on its grounds. In 1860, $125,000 had been allocated to begin work on the huge building, which would eventually become the largest hand-cut stone masonry building in North America.

While Virginia seceded from the Union in April of 1861, the state's pro-Union residents, most of them from its western counties, held a convention in Wheeling to discuss the possibility of forming a breakaway state loyal to Washington. As an interim measure, convention delegates voted on June 20, 1861, to establish a loyal government of Virginia, with Francis Pierpont of Fairmont serving as its governor. President Abraham Lincoln quickly recognized this new "restored" government as Virginia's legitimate governing body.

A few days before Tyler and his troops arrived in Weston, the Virginia Assembly in Richmond passed a resolution calling for work on the hospital to cease, and that all unspent construction funds—the thirty thousand dollars in gold being held in the Exchange Bank—be returned to Richmond for use in the war effort. When word of this development reached Weston, Union partisans alerted Presley Hale, one of Lewis County's delegates to the Wheeling Convention.

Hale urged Pierpont to seize the thirty thousand dollars before the Confederates could get their hands on it. Pierpont concurred with Hale's thinking, and urged him to board a train to Grafton to meet with Union General George B. McClellan to set a plan in motion to divert the money from the Weston bank into the "restored" state's treasury in Wheeling.

McClellan ordered Tyler, a fur merchant in western Virginia before the war, to take his regiment by rail to Clarksburg, then immediately march on to Weston, nearly twenty miles to the south.

Once there, Tyler was to confiscate the gold "by force if necessary," and "ship it to Gov. Pierpont in Wheeling," McClellan wrote in his orders, which he punctuated by ending them with a "Hurrah for New Virginia!"

While McClellan's "New Virginia" didn't stick, Tyler adhered to his orders.

Tyler and his troops arrived at the rail depot in Clarksburg on the night of June 29 and marched through the darkness to reach Weston at daybreak.

When Robert J. McCandlish, the chief operating officer and head cashier of the Weston branch of the Exchange Bank, responded to pounding on his door prior to the customary opening hour, Captain List and two rifle-toting enlisted men greeted him. He was ordered to enter the vault and hand over the construction funds, which were reportedly stored in leather bags secured with drawstrings.

McCandlish, a Union sympathizer, did not take issue with handing over the money, rifles or no rifles. But he did apparently convince the federal troops to let him keep $2,400 of the fund that was obligated to local suppliers and laborers. In addition to his banking duties, McCandlish served on the hospital's state-appointed construction oversight committee.

List and his men loaded the gold coins into a wagon and drove it back to the hospital grounds.

The following day, the 7th Ohio followed Pierpont's directive to take the money to Wheeling, the new government's temporary capital, "on behalf of its rightful owners, the true and lawful government of Virginia." On July 1, the gold coins were taken to Clarksburg, transferred onto a railcar, and eventually deposited in a Wheeling bank.

While some of the funds were used to pay for expenses incurred by the new restored government, a vote was taken in 1862 to reallocate the construction fund to the tune of forty thousand dollars and resume work on the building. Work continued after West Virginia achieved statehood on June 20, 1863, with the first section of the hospital completed and occupied by patients in October of 1864.

The hospital complex, later renamed Weston State Hospital, eventually housed up to twelve hundred patients. After 130 years of use, the hospital closed in 1994. Now privately owned under its original name, the Trans-Allegheny Lunatic Asylum is a tourist attraction, catering to visitors interested in experiencing alleged paranormal activity taking place within its timeworn walls.

ROBERT E. LEE GETS A RIDE—AND AN IMAGE

1861

In October of 1861, General Robert E. Lee, the commander of Confederate troops in the mountains of what is now West Virginia, had little to be happy about. The leaden skies above his encampment atop Sewell Mountain were as gray as the beard he had begun to cultivate, and as bleak as the prospects he imagined for his military future.

After three months of failure in a campaign to wrest control of the Staunton-Parkersburg Turnpike and the Baltimore and Ohio Railroad from Union hands, Lee found himself under attack by Southern newspaper editors and politicians, as well a larger and better equipped federal force.

"Outwitted, outmaneuvered and out-generaled," wrote an editorialist for the *Richmond Examiner* after learning that Lee was being recalled to Richmond for reassignment. Other newspapers referred to him as "Granny Lee" for what was seen as a lack of military decisiveness, or the "Great Entrencher" for having more success at building earthworks to protect his troops than at attacking the enemy.

Although Lee, at this early stage of the war, was handicapped by feuding officers within his command and troops who were more poorly supplied than their Union counterparts, there was some justification for such criticism.

The first attack Lee planned and directed as a Confederate officer, the September 12 Battle of Cheat Mountain, ended in defeat, and in its aftermath, the southern general was almost captured and his son nearly killed. Lee's complex, five-pronged assault of five thousand men on a fort and encampment near the 4,100-foot summit of Cheat Mountain fizzled in a drenching rain after the leader of one of his columns was fired upon by a small contingent from the Union garrison, eliminating the element of surprise for the Confederate troops and triggering a panicked retreat.

The following morning, Lee and a small entourage of staff officers emerged from a hayfield south of Huttonsville, where they had camped the night, and were about to steer their horses onto a well-traveled country road as a squadron of federal cavalrymen galloped by, ignoring them to pursue a larger body of Confederate stragglers. Had the cavalrymen recognized Lee and his soggy party as the command element of the rebel force, their capture could have hastened the end of the war.

Later that day, Lee dispatched his son, Major W. H. Fitzhugh Lee, on a scouting trip to make note of Union positions in the vicinity. The younger Lee was accompanied by his father's aide de camp, Lieutenant Colonel John A. Washington, a great-grandnephew of the first US president, who had only recently sold his family's Mount Vernon estate. From a hilltop just west of a federal encampment near the town of Elkwater, Lee and Washington spotted a lone mounted Union soldier and spurred their horses to intercept and capture him, not seeing a party of Indiana infantrymen emerging from a nearby wooded slope. The infantry troops fired on the two Confederate horsemen, killing Washington and shooting Lee's horse out from under him. Major Lee managed to climb atop Washington's horse and ride to safety.

At Sewell Mountain, which forms the boundary separating Fayette and Greenbrier counties, Lee had accumulated a force of about nine thousand troops and was itching for another fight. But this time, rather than take his fight to the enemy, Lee was hopeful that a similar-sized force the Union had gathered at nearby Gauley Bridge would bring the fight to him at his well-defended strongpoint. Lee was convinced that if the federal troops attacked, they lacked the reserve of supplies needed to sustain an offensive and would eventually be driven back into the Kanawha Valley. A victory here would make the long ride back to Richmond for reassignment a bit more tolerable.

As he waited for the Union force to make its move, Lee checked the positions of his troops and tried, when possible, to find a few moments of shelter from persistent rains. On one such occasion, he noticed a major in the 3rd Virginia Infantry riding past him on an iron gray gelding with a black mane and tail and a springy gait.

"When he first saw this horse, he took a great fancy to it," Thomas L. Broun of Charleston, the officer whom Lee saw riding the horse, recalled after the war. "He called it his colt, and said that he would use it before the war was over."

At Sewell Mountain, whenever Lee spotted Major Broun, or his brother, Captain Joseph Broun, riding the spirited four-year-old, "He had something pleasant to say about 'my colt,' as he designated this horse," Thomas Broun recalled.

The horse had been raised at the Greenbrier County community of Blue Sulphur Springs by farmer Andrew Johnston and was the blue-ribbon winner in 1859 and 1860 at the Greenbrier County Fair. He was owned by Johnston's son, Captain James Johnston, after the Civil War broke out and was given the name Jeff Davis, in honor of the Confederate president.

Although federal troops approached within a few miles of Lee's Sewell Mountain position in early October, they withdrew to the Kanawha Valley on the night of October 5, giving Lee no further reason for lingering in the highlands of what was then western Virginia.

As fate would have it, both Lee and Captain Joseph Broun would be reassigned to the low country of South Carolina in February of 1862. Lee was in charge of the placement and construction of coastal defenses, while Broun was quartermaster for a Virginia infantry unit assigned to the project.

"Upon seeing my brother on this horse, General Lee at once recognized the horse and again inquired pleasantly about 'his' colt," Broun said in a postwar newspaper interview. The captain offered the horse, which the Broun brothers had named Greenbrier, to the general as a gift, which Lee declined. Joseph Broun countered by offering to sell the horse to the general at cost, which Lee accepted, adding $25 to make up for inflation.

General Lee renamed the horse Traveller, and the Greenbrier County steed remained his mount of choice throughout the war and into the postwar years. Traveller outlived his master and walked behind Lee's funeral caisson following his death in 1870. The following year, Traveller developed tetanus after stepping on a nail and died. He was buried outside Lee Chapel on the campus of Washington & Lee University, a short distance from Robert E. Lee's final resting place. Atop a stone marking the horse's grave, students and visitors leave coins for good luck.

It was during his trying time as a commander in the mountains of what is now West Virginia in 1861 that Lee grew his trademark beard, which he wore through the remainder of the war. The gray-bearded southern general perched atop his iron gray steed was the subject of numerous photographs, paintings, and drawings during the course of the war. It's an image with deep West Virginia roots.

THE GOLDEN BOUGH

1905

While walking through the apple orchard overlooking Porter Creek on his family's thirty-six-acre farm in the autumn of 1905, Anderson Mullins noticed a young tree bearing large yellow apples in an area a short distance away from the familiar grove of trees he and his relatives had planted.

Since no yellow apple varieties had been planted in his orchard, Mullins speculated that the young tree must have sprouted from a seed carried to the site by a bird or other animal. He sampled the golden fruit and found that it had a sweet, slightly spicy taste and a firm texture.

In the months that followed, he learned that the yellow apple kept its shape, taste, moistness, and crispness through the winter storage period, and made an excellent primary ingredient in pies, applesauce, and apple butter. The young tree bearing the fruit out-produced the orchard trees raised from nursery stock, and it did well even during periods of drought. He named the "volunteer" tree the Mullins Yellow Seedling.

As fruit from the Mullins Yellow Seedling became popular with the residents of the Porter Creek communities of Odessa, Glen, and Bomont in Clay County, Mullins realized he was in possession of something special. In the spring of 1914, he mailed a box containing three of his locally famous yellow apples and a note detailing their characteristics to his primary mail-order orchard supplier, Stark Brothers Nurseries of Louisiana, Missouri.

When Paul Stark opened the box and examined the fruit, he wasn't immediately enthusiastic. Red apples were all the rage in the orchard industry, and yellow apple varieties were generally slow sellers. But Stark sliced up one of the three West Virginia apples, called in his brother, Lloyd, and sampled the fruit.

"We had never experienced such a spicy flavor before, especially from a yellow apple," Paul Stark later wrote of the first tasting. "With one in your hand, you can't be sure whether you're drinking champagne or eating an apple." Stark immediately made plans to visit Mullins' orchard during the coming apple season.

In early autumn, Stark traveled by train from his hometown in Missouri to Charleston, where he transferred to a narrow gauge railway that traveled up the Elk River to the vicinity of Queen Shoals. There, Stark hired someone to take him by horse and buggy to Odessa and Mullins' orchard.

No one answered when Stark knocked on the farmhouse door, so he wandered up the nearby hillside to the small orchard, where he spotted the tree bearing golden fruit.

"There, looming forth in the midst of small, leafless, barren trees was one tree with rich green foliage, as if it had been transplanted from the Garden of Eden," he later wrote, with a dollop or two of hyperbole, of the encounter. "That tree's boughs were bending to the ground beneath a tremendous crop of great, glorious, glowing golden apples. . . . I picked one and bit into its crisp, tender, juice-laden flesh. Eureka! I had found it!"

At about the same time that Stark sampled the apple, Mullins spotted him in the orchard and greeted him.

"That's some apple," Stark said, after identifying himself, as recalled in an article he later wrote in a Stark Brothers catalogue.

Stark paid the Mullins family what was then the princely sum of five thousand dollars for the tree and the small patch of land surrounding it, and arranged to have the tree encompassed by a thirty-foot-square woven wire cage. An electric alarm was later rigged to the cage and connected to the kitchen of the Mullins' farmhouse to discourage thieves.

Stark returned to Missouri with a bundle of scion cuttings from the tree and grafted them to trees in his apple orchard there. Among those who critiqued the fruit Stark produced from the cuttings was John Harvey Kellogg, founder of the Kellogg's cereal company, who deemed the Golden Delicious to be "the finest apple I have ever tasted."

In 1916, Stark Brothers introduced the Golden Delicious apple commercially as a companion to the Red Delicious, even though the two varieties are unrelated.

At about that time, Anderson Mullins swapped farms with his brother, Bewell, the man who planted the orchard. Bewell was hired by Stark Brothers to serve as caretaker of the tree for the next thirty years. The Golden Delicious mother tree continued to produce fruit into the 1950s.

In 1958, a pair of West Virginia University professors, hoping to find living shoots from the original tree from which to propagate nursery stock, found the lifeless remains of the former Mullins Yellow Seedling surrounded by rusty fencing. They took a few photos of the famous tree, and one of them later sketched the scene in a pen-and-ink drawing.

How did the anomaly later known as the first Golden Delicious apple tree come into being?

One theory is that the tree was the naturally occurring hybrid of a French Reinette—a yellow apple variety occasionally planted in West Virginia in the early 1900s—and a Golden Grimes apple. The Golden Grimes is another anomalous West Virginia original, with its first known occurrence identified in the early 1800s near Wellsburg in Brooke County. The relatively popular Golden Grimes was, and is, a smaller, tougher-skinned variety than the Golden Delicious and was planted widely.

According to that theory, a bird that dined on a French Reinette apple that had been fertilized by a Golden Grimes traveled to the Mullins's farm, and deposited the seed that would become the world's first Golden Delicious during a rest stop there.

Today, the Golden Delicious is one of the world's most popular apple varieties and is grown from England to Tasmania. By the time the West Virginia Legislature designated it the Official State Fruit of West Virginia in 1995, nearly two hundred billion pounds of the variety were grown annually in the United States.

A historical marker along State Secondary Route 1 near the former Mullins farm gives travelers a brief description of the tree and its history.

Since 1973, the Clay County Golden Delicious Apple Festival has been held each September, featuring baking contests, apple butter–making demonstrations, traditional music, an antique car show, and a beauty pageant.

EXPLOSION UNDERGROUND

1907

At 10:30 on a bright December morning, the business of mining coal seemed to be proceeding as normal at Fairmont Coal Company's Monongah No. 6 mine, one of the most productive mines in the nation's most abundant coal state. Far beneath the ground, hundreds of men and boys, some as young as eight, pursued the backbreaking work of loading coal into mine cars by hand or performing ancillary tasks like carrying water, tools, or supplies.

A. H. Leonard watched as a series of nineteen interconnected mine cars, each loaded with three tons of coal, emerged from the portal of Fairmont Coal Company's Monongah No. 6 mine and headed for the four-hundred-foot-long trestle that would carry them across the West Fork River to a processing plant and rail loading facility.

It was a sight that was seen repeatedly on any given working day at the huge underground coal mine, where Leonard's job was to keep the mine's huge ventilation fan, capable of moving 350,000 cubic feet of air per minute, lubricated and its belts and pulleys tight. As Leonard walked toward the fan to begin a routine oiling, he noticed that the first car out of the mine was hung up on the "knuckle" connecting the track leading out of the mine with the track on the trestle. In addition to his fan maintenance duties, it was Leonard's job to trip a derailing switch in the event of such a mine car jam-up, to prevent the mine cars from plunging back down the thirteen-hundred-foot slope into the mine—and into the people who worked there. But before Leonard could make it to the switch, the unthinkable happened: A coupling pin snapped, and the nineteen cars and nearly sixty tons of coal plummeted backward into the mine, ripping out wiring, ventilation curtains, and support timbers as they descended into darkness.

When the mine cars and the avalanche of debris they dislodged hit bottom, a blast of air was forced back into the mine entryways, playing havoc with the ventilation system deep in the mine and causing explosive coal dust and volatile methane to swirl into the shaft. In an instant, a rumbling could be heard deep in the No. 6 mine, which was connected underground to Fairmont Coal's Monongah No. 8 mine, though their entryways were a half-mile apart. An instant later, fire, dust, and debris shot out of the No. 6 mine, knocking Leonard off his feet and covering him with rubble.

A few moments later, a second explosion rocked the West Fork valley, sending fire, timbers, and obliterated mining gear out of the No. 8 mine's portal. The ten-ton, thirty-foot-tall ventilation fan that forced air deep into the No. 8 mine was sent rocketing across the West Fork, where it cratered into a hillside a half-mile from its mounting. The mine's powerhouse was obliterated, as was a one-hundred-foot chunk of mountainside surrounding the portal.

The explosions could be heard for miles, instantly alerting the miners' family members and off-duty colleagues that disaster had struck. Within minutes, crowds began to form at the entrances to the mines, along with off-duty miners anxious to mount rescue operations.

Although European coal mines had made use of specially trained rescue teams for decades, coal miners in the United States relied on spur-of-the-moment, seat-of-the pants responses to mine disasters.

Outside the No. 6 mine, "terror stricken women were tearing their hair from their heads by the handfuls and sinking fingernails deep into their faces," according to a newspaper account of the disaster. "They demanded to know the fate of their loved ones but it was impossible to tell them anything."

In nearby Fairmont, Monongah No. 6 miner Perry Vernon organized a rescue crew and commandeered a street car to carry them to the mine entrance, where they arrived about twenty-five minutes after the blast. No mine officials could immediately be found, and it was unknown whether the mine was on fire or filled with lethal gas. As the rescuers discussed how to proceed with the recovery effort, four miners who had been working near a rock outcrop that provided a natural vent to the surface emerged from the opening dazed and bleeding but otherwise unhurt. The shaken miners could tell rescuers nothing about the cause of the blast, the extent of damage, or the fate of the hundreds of other miners still underground.

At the No. 8 portal, rescuers cleared away debris blocking the entrance to the main shaft and forced their way into the mine, only to encounter a toxic mine gas called "black damp." Several of the rescuers were overcome by the gas and had to be rescued themselves. A fan was brought in to replace the one hurled across the West Fork during the explosion, and the rescue parties slowly advanced, using canvas curtains to restore ventilation as they ventured deeper into the mine.

At the bottom of the No. 6 mine's entry slope, rescuers were nearly blocked by the wreckage of the nineteen mine cars that Leonard saw plummeting into the shaft just before the explosion. Outside the mine, more than five hours after the blast, a rescue party walking past an outcrop hole could hear moaning from inside the mine. Using a rope, they lowered a man into the mine shaft, one hundred feet below, where Polish-American miner Peter Urban was found sitting on the body of his brother. Urban, who was sobbing inconsolably, was staring vacantly into space. Later, Urban told rescuers he heard the first explosion, but his brother did not, telling him, "I don't think anything happened." But after the second explosion rocked the mine, the Urban brothers began running toward the portal, which they never reached. Rescuers had no way of knowing it then, but Urban was the last man found alive in either of the mines.

As exhausted rescue crews climbed over rubble, breathed in dangerous gases that produced headaches and nausea, and suffered through intense heat, they encountered the bodies of hundreds of their friends and co-workers, and painstakingly carried their remains thousands of feet back to the mine portals. A temporary morgue was set up in the company-owned First National Bank of Monongah. Funeral homes in the Fairmont area quickly sold all of the coffins they had in stock. Across the Ohio River in Zanesville, Ohio, the Muskingum Coffin Company went into emergency production, working around the clock to meet the demand for new coffins. At one point, a crowd panicked the horses bearing one wagon load of freshly filled coffins from the morgue. The wagon overturned, tossing bodies of coal miners into the street as the team ran headlong into the West Fork.

In Monongah and Fairmont, embalmers worked around the clock to keep pace with the volume of bodies being recovered and churches held several funeral services each day. Identification of the bodies was made difficult due to the extreme injuries many miners received in the blast, and to the fact that the boards used to post the names of miners working in the mines were vaporized by the explosions. Many of those working in the Monongah mines on December 6 were subcontractors, working in the place of company-paid miners, and paid by the miners for whom they were substituting—a common practice at the time. The company did not keep track of such workers.

After six days of rescue and recovery work, the bodies of 320 miners had been found. The remains that could be identified were embalmed and dressed in black suits, courtesy of the coal company. Unidentified bodies and body fragments were taken directly from the mine portals to a new cemetery dug in a bleak hillside surrounded by company-owned miners' homes, where they were immediately interred.

While the official death count for the Monongah Mine Disaster was 362, new estimates taking subcontractors into account place the death toll at more than five hundred. The disaster left more than one thousand women and children without husbands and fathers. Of thirty houses on Camden Avenue in Monongah, twenty-seven did not have a man left in them after the explosions.

Teams of investigators from Ohio, West Virginia, and Pennsylvania attempted to determine the cause of the explosion, resulting in mixed findings. Fairmont Coal president C. W. Watson told a *New York Times* reporter that the explosion was likely caused by an accumulation of coal dust, possibly ignited by a miner's careless use of an open lamp.

Clarence Hall of the US Commerce Department, who had looked into the Monongah blast and a series of deadly explosions that preceded it, said, "It cannot be claimed that all these explosions are due to the carelessness of the miners. We know so little about how these explosions occur."

The mine accident investigation team from Ohio concluded that the mine train plunging backward into the mine dislodged volatile gases and raised clouds of coal dust, which were ignited by an unknown source—possibly a blown-out blasting shot. Whatever the cause of the blast, the fact that the two mines were connected underground doubled its impact, and doubled the number of dead.

The year 1907 was the deadliest year for coal miners in US history. By the time the last bodies had been pulled out of the Monongah mines, a total of 3,242 miners across the nation's coalfields had perished.

"If the general conditions of the operating mines in the various states are not soon covered by adequate federal laws, the sacrifice of human life in the mines has merely just begun," the report issued by the Ohio investigation team on the Monongah Mine Disaster concluded. "More men are killed in the state of West Virginia than any other state in the Union, or country in the world. Where the men have no organization, the mine operators pay little or no attention to the law, generally speaking."

Fallout from the Monongah Mine Disaster is credited with spurring the creation of the US Bureau of Mines in 1910, which began the development of mine safety training programs, the certification of safe and reliable mine equipment, and official investigations into the causes of mine accidents.

ROUGHING IT WITH
THE VAGABONDS

1918, 1921

One of the earliest groups of tourists to use the automobile to access West Virginia's scenic mountain camping locales was the Vagabonds, whose members included auto magnate Henry Ford, inventor Thomas Edison, tire tycoon Harvey Firestone, and an occasional US president.

Annual road trips by the Vagabonds and their entourage of drivers, cooks, Secret Service agents, newspaper reporters, and newsreel photographers got their start in 1914, when Ford and Edison and their families drove into Florida's Everglades in search of summer adventure. The following year, the Vagabonds toured Southern California, traveling the roads between Los Angeles and San Diego.

The Vagabonds expanded their itinerary for their 1918 tour, which consisted of a southward sweep into the Appalachians from Pennsylvania into West Virginia, Virginia, and Maryland, and on into the Smoky Mountains of Tennessee and North Carolina.

West Virginia stops included the steep, densely forested mountains of Tucker County and the community of Leadmine, where in August of 1918, Edison, Ford, Firestone, and naturalist John Burroughs posed on the huge water wheel of the Evans Gristmill and in the cab of a log train locomotive. After camping out along Horseshoe Run in the Leadmine area and buying a bushel of apples from a local girl, the Vagabonds motored on to Keysers Ridge near Parsons, where they took in a picnic lunch in a rail-fenced pasture and sacked out for a shady siesta under a towering oak tree.

From there, they drove on to Elkins and proceeded east, follow-ing back roads that crisscrossed Shavers Fork of Cheat River until they reached the Cheat Mountain Club, a remote hunting lodge shaded by red spruce trees at an elevation of more than four thousand feet.

"The people at the big clubhouse gave us a hospitable welcome and added much to our comfort," Burroughs wrote. "I found the forests and streams of this part of West Virginia much like those of the Catskills, only on a larger scale, and the climate even colder. That night [July 23, 1918] the mercury dropped to thirty. On July 24th they had frost that killed all their garden truck."

Burroughs said paper outlines of big trout caught by Cheat Mountain Club members lined the walls of the lodge's main room. "Evidently 'Cheat River' deserves a better name," he observed.

From Cheat Mountain, the Vagabonds' caravan traveled to the southeast, stopping at an oat field near Bartow where they watched a farmer mowing oats with a handheld cradle scythe. Ford and Firestone borrowed the implement and had their pictures taken attempting to duplicate the farmer's work.

One of the photographs "shows the farmer and Mr. Ford looking on with broad smiles, watching Mr. Firestone with the fingers of the cradle tangled in the oats and weeds, a smile on his face also, but decidedly an equivocal smile," Burroughs wrote. "The trick was not as easy as it looked."

The Vagabonds passed through White Sulphur Springs in Greenbrier County and Sweet Springs in Monroe County before proceeding through Virginia into North Carolina.

"I think to most of us West Virginia had always been a rather hazy proposition, and we were glad to get a clearer impression of it," Burroughs wrote. "A beautiful spot," Edison wrote in the Cheat Mountain Club's guest register.

While the vagabonds did camp out on their motor trips, their version of roughing it included traveling in two chauffeur-driven Packards, while their staff of seven servants and cooks traveled in two Model T Fords and two Ford trucks crammed with camping gear and supplies.

One of the two trucks in the caravan was used exclusively to carry food and kitchen gear. Iceboxes in the truck kept the Vagabonds supplied with steaks, ham, bacon, and vegetables, while fresh eggs, milk, and cream were bought from farmers along their route.

Each Vagabond slept on a cot in his own ten-foot-square tent, equipped with mosquito netting and an embroidered panel bearing the occupant's name. A four-hundred-square-foot dining tent was erected nearby, in which a circular, nine-foot-diameter dining table was placed. At the center of the table, a large, rotating "Lazy Suzan" platter was placed, allowing diners to easily reach condiments and side dishes. Surrounding the table was a series of then new-fangled collapsible wood and canvas chairs.

A large gas stove was used to prepare some meals, but the Vagabonds preferred their food to be cooked on an iron grill suspended over a campfire.

Ford chopped wood for the campfires and occasionally tried his hand at flipping breakfast flapjacks, but a professional chef handled the bulk of the group's food preparation chores. While Ford and Edison enjoyed bathing in woodland streams, Firestone preferred the comfort and convenience of hotel room bathing, and deferred his full-body contacts with soap and water until reaching the nearest sizeable town.

An entourage of newspaper reporters and photographers and newsreel cameramen often accompanied the Vagabonds on segments of their journeys.

During the summer of 1921, the Vagabonds made their final tour through West Virginia, minus Burroughs, who died earlier in the year. They traveled from Oakland, Maryland, to Elkins, where they waited out a downpour in a hotel before traveling back roads to the east to reach their campsite along Shavers Fork of Cheat River on August 1. But that encampment was short-lived. After only a day in the mountains, both Ford and Firestone received messages that they had to return to their offices immediately to take care of urgent business.

They broke camp on August 2 and drove through Fairmont and Morgantown before crossing into Pennsylvania and heading for points east. Their summer tours continued for another three summers but never involved a return to West Virginia.

During the early part of their 1921 trip, President Warren Harding briefly joined the Vagabonds. As the industrialists and the president traveled along a muddy West Virginia road somewhere between Elkins and the Maryland border, the Lincoln in which they were riding bogged down in the mire.

According to a *Detroit News* account of the incident, Ford's chauffeur slogged his way to a nearby farm and returned with a farmer driving a Model T Ford, who managed to pull the Lincoln to solid ground.

"I guess you don't know me, but I'm Henry Ford," the automaker reportedly told the Good Samaritan. "I made the car you're driving."

Firestone then pointed toward the Model T's wheels and identified himself as "the man who made those tires," and introduced the remaining two of the remaining three occupants of the car as "the man who invented the electric light and the president of the United States."

Finally, agriculturalist Luther Burbank, the fifth man in the Lincoln, shook the farmer's hand, saying, "I guess you don't know me, either."

"No," the farmer responded. "But if you're the same kind of liar as these other darned fools, I wouldn't be surprised if you said you was Santa Claus."

BLAIR MOUNTAIN BOMB THREAT

1921

General Billy Mitchell, the commander of all US air operations in Europe during World War I, brought his DeHavilland DH-4B bomber to a gentle landing at newly built Kanawha Field just east of Charleston on August 26, 1921, eager to demonstrate a new unconventional use of air power—quelling an American labor dispute.

In July, Mitchell had successfully shown that the bombers were capable of sinking large warships from high altitude by sending a captured German battleship to the bottom of the Atlantic off the coast of Virginia in a demonstration for Pentagon officials.

In West Virginia, he hoped to show the nation's top military brass more air power versatility by sending the same squadron of bombers that sank the German battleship the previous month to the mountains of Appalachia to scuttle what was becoming the largest civil uprising in America since the Civil War.

Mitchell, the assistant chief of the Army Air Corps, had been summoned to West Virginia by President Warren Harding, on behalf of Governor Ephraim Morgan, as events in the state's simmering Mine Wars began to boil over. Miners seeking to better their lives through union representation had been fired from their jobs, evicted from their company-owned homes, and sometimes beaten or shot at by coal company thugs. Meanwhile, mine operators assembled armies of hired guns and anti-union sheriff's deputies, rigged locomotives with armor plating and machine guns, and began stockpiling munitions in preparation for a battle in the state's southern coalfields, where tensions on both sides were feverish.

"All of this could be left up to the air service," the trim, graying Mitchell told reporters after climbing out of his DeHavilland at Kanawha Field decked out in spurs and a flight suit rigged with a gun belt and sidearm, plus two rows of campaign ribbons. "If I get orders, I can move in the necessary forces in three hours."

"We believe we are in for a little of the kind of warfare we once thought was coming to us in Mexico—getting small bands of bushwhackers out from impregnable mountain passes," one of Mitchell's officers said in another interview.

When a reporter asked how he would subdue the miners, Mitchell responded with a single word: "Gas," he said. "You understand, we wouldn't try to kill people at first," he elaborated. "We'd drop gas all over the place. If they refused to disperse, we'd open up with artillery preparation and everything."

After determining that Kanawha Field was capable of accommodating bombers, he ordered members of the Eighty-eighth Air Squadron to report for service in Charleston with seventeen DeHavilland DH-4 and four Martin MB-2 bombers. Army officials in Washington, DC, ordered a large quantity of 150-pound tear gas bombs, "guaranteed to incapacitate within three hundred yards," sent by rail to Charleston.

Meanwhile, in coal rich Logan County, Sheriff Don Chafin, using funds from the Logan Coal Operators Association, had already assembled a small air force of three private biplanes, as well as a much larger army of men—about two thousand in all—to block a march by more than five thousand miners from the Kanawha Valley to the coalfields of Logan and Mingo Counties.

Earlier that year, Sid Hatfield, the chief of police in the Mingo County town of Matewan, confronted a group of coal company detectives illegally evicting miners and their families from their homes and attempted to place them under arrest. When they refused, Hatfield, a group of deputized townspeople, and the town's mayor engaged them in a gunfight, during which ten men died, including the mayor and two high-ranking members of the Baldwin-Felts Detective Agency. On August 1, as Hatfield and a friend were preparing to enter the McDowell County Courthouse in Welch, they were ambushed and gunned down by a party of Baldwin-Felts operatives. No attempt was made by authorities to bring Hatfield's assassins to justice.

Hatfield's unpunished murder served as a rallying point for union-leaning miners across the southern coalfields.

By August 29, a battle line had been drawn along the ridgeline of Blair Mountain, which straddles the border between Logan and Boone Counties. While the miner's force, armed with hunting rifles and handguns, was larger than Chafin's, the Logan sheriff's force was better equipped and occupied the higher ground.

Over the miners' positions, Chafin's three-plane air force dropped leaflets carrying a proclamation by Governor Morgan ordering them to lay down their arms and return home. After the leaflets were ignored, Chafin's biplanes returned, this time dropping two-foot-long homemade pipe bombs crammed with explosives and rigged with stabilizing fins on the coal mining communities of Jeffrey, Sharples, and Blair along the Boone-Logan border. Many of the bombs failed to detonate, and those that did explode caused no injuries.

Mitchell, though itching to join the fight, was ordered back to Washington by Army officials who had tired of his incendiary statements. The aircrews of the Eighty-eighth Air Squadron performed six reconnaissance missions, all in unarmed aircraft, occasionally drawing rifle fire from the miners below.

After a week of skirmishing, during which about fifty men were killed and hundreds more injured, federal troops arrived to disarm the warring parties, ending the bloody standoff at Blair Mountain.

Use of the Army bombers during the action accounted for the only time in US history that military aircraft had participated in a civil disturbance. Mitchell, though disappointed that his plans to drop tear gas bombs fell through, said he was generally pleased with the air squadron's performance in the operation. He said the Eighty-eighth's mission provided "an excellent example of the potentialities of air power—that we can go wherever there is air."

Observers lacking Mitchell's unwavering enthusiasm for air power may have analyzed the mission differently.

On the squadron's flight from Langley Field, Virginia, to Charleston, a refueling stop was made at Roanoke, Virginia. After taking off there for the final leg of the journey to Charleston, one of the DeHavillands clipped a telephone pole and crashed, destroying the aircraft but not seriously injuring its two-man crew. Two other bombers failed to make the Roanoke-Charleston flight due to mechanical problems, while another DeHavilland developed engine trouble in flight and broke an axle making an emergency landing near Beckley. Two other bomber crews got lost in the clouds after departing Roanoke and diverted to Mooresburg, Tennessee. Attempting to reach Charleston the following day, one struck a ditch while making an emergency landing in a field, destroying the aircraft's landing gear, while the other crash-landed on a hillside near Beckley and burst into flames. None of the crew members was seriously injured in any of those incidents.

While flying reconnaissance missions out of Charleston, another bomber's landing gear collapsed, while another DeHavilland broke an axle making an emergency landing near Narrows, Virginia.

Of the four Martin bombers flown in from Aberdeen, Maryland, to join the squadron, one struck a fence and crashed while attempting an emergency landing near Fairmont. Its crew escaped injury. Another Martin crew wasn't as lucky. Shortly after departing Charleston at the end of the operation, it was seen banking sharply to the left as it approached the town of Summersville and then spiraling to the ground in a nosedive. It took search crews two days to find the wreckage on a hillside near Drennen. Miraculously, one crewman, Corporal Alexander Hazelton of Wilmington, Delaware, was still alive, and though severely injured, survived the ordeal. The other three crew members died on impact. The crash site and remaining wreckage are believed to have been destroyed after a surface coal mine opened in the vicinity several decades ago.

The Blair Mountain battle site is also threatened by surface mining. The State of West Virginia, acting on behalf of landowners, has petitioned the Department of the Interior to remove a section of Blair Mountain's Spruce Fork Ridge that had been listed on the National Register of Historic Places in 2008. Two coal companies have been issued permits to surface-mine coal from much of the site. In June of 2011, hundreds of battlefield preservationists and anti-mountaintop-removal-mining activists marched to Blair Mountain from Charleston to protest the possible obliteration of the battle site.

TRAINING AIRMEN FOR TUSKEGEE

1939

As a teenager growing up in Fairmont during the 1930s, George S. Roberts enjoyed watching airplanes take off and land at the small airport near his family's home, sometimes imagining himself at the controls of a sky-bound aircraft.

The prospects of making such a daydream a reality were virtually impossible for an African-American youth like Roberts, even as America's involvement in World War II approached and the need for military pilots became dire. But Roberts was a man determined to beat the odds and realize his dream—not only to fly, but to fly fighter planes for the Army Air Corps. After graduating from Fairmont's all-black Dunbar High School at age fifteen, Roberts enrolled at West Virginia State College in Institute, one of six historically black colleges in the nation to offer a new Civilian Pilot Training Program. In 1939, there were only 125 licensed African-American pilots in the United States.

On November 14, 1939, after earning a degree in mechanical engineering at the age of eighteen, Roberts became a member of West

Virginia State's first Civilian Pilot Training Program class, through which he received seventy-two hours of classroom instruction and thirty-five hours of flight time at Wertz Field, Charleston's municipal airport, conveniently located on an expanse of flat land adjacent to West Virginia State's campus. By the summer of 1940, Roberts had soloed and earned his civilian wings. A total of 110 students earned their wings through Civilian Pilot Training at West Virginia State before the program was phased out in 1943.

While Roberts was willing to put his flying skills to use in the Army Air Corps, America's military establishment at that time was rife with racial stereotyping and unwilling to accommodate him and other black Civilian Pilot Training graduates. In June of 1941, President Franklin D. Roosevelt signed an executive order that barred all branches of the armed forces from excluding blacks. But instead of fully integrating their ranks, the War Department hierarchy chose to create all-black units, which were often given supply and maintenance tasks rather than combat roles.

A rare exception to that model was the 99th Fighter Squadron, an Army Air Corps unit being organized and trained at Tuskegee Institute in Alabama, one of the six black schools offering the Civilian Pilot Training Program. Roberts became the first cadet to enter fighter pilot training with the Tuskegee unit, making him the first African-American cadet accepted for pilot training in the Army Air Corps.

Nearly all the pilot trainees for the 99th were Civilian Pilot Training Program alumni. Thirty-three graduates of the West Virginia State College program went on to become Tuskegee Airmen.

Determined to make the 99th a success, its leaders were tough on trainees. Of the thirteen cadets who entered the unit's first pilot training program in July, 1941, only five graduated, including Roberts and another West Virginia State alumnus, Mac Ross of Dayton, Ohio. On March 7, 1942, Roberts was commissioned a second lieutenant at Tuskegee Air Field. During a runway ceremony following the commissioning rite, Roberts married his West Virginia State College classmate, Edith McMillan.

After serving as a trainer in an advanced flight school at Tuskegee, Roberts was named commander of the 99th Fighter Squadron. The unit shipped out for North Africa in May 1943 and began flying missions against German and Italian aircraft and ground targets in P-40 War Hawks. Roberts later became commander of the 322nd fighter group, made up of four squadrons of black aviators and began flying bomber escort missions over Europe using P-47 Thunderbolt and P-51 Mustang fighter planes. He ended the war with more than one hundred combat missions under his belt, with the Tuskegee Airmen of the 322nd shooting down 112 enemy aircraft in aerial combat and destroying 150 more on the ground. Of the 922 pilots who completed the training program at Tuskegee, 450 were shipped overseas, where 150 of them were killed in action or accidents.

After President Harry Truman ordered all branches of the military to end the use of racially segregated units in 1948, Roberts was transferred to Langley Air Force Base in Virginia and became the first African-American to command a racially integrated unit in the US Air Force. He later qualified as a jet fighter pilot and commanded a fighter group in Korea. During the 1960s, as a full colonel, he oversaw all ground radar systems for the Air Force and served as deputy chief of logistics for the Air Force's fighter program in Vietnam.

After logging more than six thousand hours of military flight time and retiring from the Air Force in 1968, Roberts became a banker in Sacramento, California. He died in 1984.

In 1999, a new highway span in Fairmont was named the George S. "Spanky" Roberts Bridge in honor of the hometown Tuskegee Airman.

NUCLEAR DAWN

1943

In January of 1943, the sprawling Morgantown Ordnance Works was already heavily involved in producing munitions to feed the Allies' war machine in its battle against Axis forces when it was given a new, secret mission.

Built in less than one year, the 825-acre factory began producing its first batch of synthetic ammonia for use in high explosives on December 7, 1941—just a few hours after the Japanese launched their surprise raid on Pearl Harbor. Working around the clock in eight-hour shifts, the factory's fourteen hundred employees produced the components needed to arm torpedoes, artillery shells, mines, and other lethal implements of war.

The plant's constantly burning coke ovens cast a perpetual glow over Morgantown's night skies. Unbeknownst to those who toiled in its shadow, the factory was about to play a role in ushering in the dawn of the nuclear age.

On December 2, 1942, a team of scientists led by Enrico Fermi successfully initiated a nuclear chain reaction in a secret lab in what was once a University of Chicago squash court as part of their work with the Manhattan Project, America's top-secret effort to develop the world's first atomic bomb.

Later that month, President Franklin D. Roosevelt, encouraged by Fermi's success, ordered General Leslie Groves, head of the Manhattan Project, to proceed with the development of three possible methods to produce nuclear materials. To comply with FDR's directive, Groves needed to dramatically increase the nation's supply of heavy water, which was in extremely short supply.

Heavy water, or deuterium oxide, first developed in 1932, has twice the mass and weight of ordinary hydrogen. It was needed for use as a moderating agent to contain experimental nuclear pile reactions being designed by Manhattan Project engineers.

When the United States entered World War II, it produced no heavy water. Manhattan Project researchers initially relied on a small supply of deuterium oxide being produced by a factory in the Canadian province of British Columbia. The Canadian factory produced about one-half ton of heavy water annually, but the Manhattan Project needed at least three tons of the substance a year to proceed with its nuclear development plans.

In January of 1942, Groves ordered three armament factories associated with DuPont, whose engineers were already involved with Manhattan Project research, to begin secretly producing heavy water. One of them was operating at the Morgantown Ordnance Works, while the other DuPont operations were located in the Wabash River Ordnance Works in Newport, Indiana, and the Alabama Ordnance Works in Sylacauga, Alabama.

While DuPont workers operated the machinery that produced conventional weapons components at the three plants, the heavy water additions to the factories would be built and operated by Corps of Engineers personnel to cover security concerns. To avoid

Congressional attention, the new heavy water plants were paid for by adding funding supplements to existing DuPont munitions contracts.

While key Army Corps of Engineers officials were aware of the heavy water plants on a need-to-know basis, all other military organizations were left out of the loop. That included the Army's Ordnance Department, which, according to the Manhattan Project hierarchy, was explicitly "not to be involved in the design or knowledge of use of the product."

The heavy water churned out by the Morgantown factory and its two sister plants was code-named "Product 9" by Manhattan Project officials, and was to be used in the production of weapons-grade plutonium in the development of an atomic bomb.

It is unlikely that more than a very few workers and administrators at the Morgantown plant were aware of the role their factory played in developing the world's first atomic bomb. Producing components for conventional weapons kept them fully occupied. In 1943, they were awarded the presidential "E" award for efficiency and productivity.

By war's end, the Morgantown plant was one of thirty research and production sites secretly affiliated with the Manhattan Project.

Two weeks after the world's first atomic bomb was dropped on Hiroshima, the Morgantown Ordnance Works was closed. Some of the West Virginia heavy water gear was later transferred to the Wabash River Ordnance Works in Indiana, where it continued to produce Product 9 for use in early Cold War weaponry.

Today, the former Morgantown Ordnance Works is an industrial and office park, housing twenty businesses and organizations, including the Make-A-Wish Foundation of Northern West Virginia.

Its secret role in the rush to develop the world's first atomic bomb remains virtually unknown.

FUNNEL VISION

1944

Floyd Pierson was taking advantage of the lingering warmth of an early summer day to set out tomato plants in his Shinnston garden when he looked across the freshly turned soil and saw a curious phenomenon: All of his honeybees had gathered in an enormous swarm and were trying to reenter the wooden hives lining the garden at the same time.

Pierson looked around for signs of a disturbance capable of triggering such a reaction and initially noticed nothing. Then he looked up. There, one hundred feet above him, a large uprooted tree was twisting silently through the sky in the early evening light, which had taken on a greenish, smoky tint.

On the south side of Shinnston, Roddy and Lily Rice watched from their porch as a black cloud of what appeared to be smoke approached their home, accompanied by a deep rumbling noise. After convincing themselves that a steam locomotive approaching Shinnston's rail yard was responsible, they retired to their living room, where Mrs. Rice continued to watch the cloud through a front window. Almost immediately she saw the tail of a tornado funnel whip down a hillside and collapse the new all-steel State Police radio tower, obliterate a wooden oil derrick, and streak up an adjacent hillside where it began consuming the fifteen wood frame homes perched on its slope.

"Roddy!" she shouted to her husband. "All those homes on South Shinnston Hill are gone!"

"You must be mistaken," he replied. But when he got up to investigate, he learned otherwise.

The almost unbroken series of hills and mountains that stretch border to border across West Virginia give residents of the state a sense of security when it comes to considering the likelihood of a tornado touching down. The idea that the state's terrain shields it from death-dealing twisters is not entirely unfounded. Before the Shinnston Tornado created its forty-mile path of destruction on June 29, 1944, leaving 103 people dead and 430 injured, only four tornadoes, which killed a total of three people, had struck West Virginia since weather data began being collected in 1874.

The Shinnston Tornado first touched down shortly after 8 p.m. in the Glade Fork community, about ten miles northwest of Shinnston. Traveling at speeds ranging between thirty and forty miles per hour, with vortex winds approaching five hundred miles per hour inside the funnel, it traveled constantly toward the southeast, cutting a swath of destruction ranging from one hundred to five hundred yards wide, until it blew itself out against the three-thousand-foot northern end of Cheat Mountain, east of Montrose in Randolph County.

In downtown Shinnston, West Virginia State Police Corporal J. B. Jack, in town to take part in a trial, was directing traffic around a blown and burning power transformer when he noticed what appeared to be a column of smoke approaching the town of three thousand. "It seemed to extend up to and connect with the heavy cloud riding overhead," he told a newspaper reporter after the storm passed. "For about one hundred feet up, the column was very black, then it tapered to a lighter color. The entire affair seemed to be going around and around in true merry-go-round fashion. It was hard to believe, here in West Virginia, but I knew I was looking at a tornado—a terrible tornado."

Jack watched, open-mouthed, as the funnel struck the Pleasant Hill neighborhood of Shinnston "and scattered houses like toys. Just a few of the houses were left standing, and they were twisted into weird shapes. The rest were utterly destroyed."

The state policeman jogged up the hill to assess the damage. "From all directions I could hear the screams of the injured, and everywhere I looked I could see half-conscious people staggering about," he recalled. "I met one man dazedly walking about, his arm fractured, and the jagged end of a bone sticking out through the skin. The saddest thing I saw was the number of men and women with children in their arms, many of them dead or dying. All victims were covered with a dirty grime—a kind of water and dirt mixture."

Some survivors said the twister vacuumed up water from the West Fork River as it passed over the stream at Shinnston, leaving the muddy river bottom exposed and visible for an instant.

With World War II still in progress, a number of people thought the town had come under attack from the air.

As she watched debris flying through the air toward her home, "I thought, the Germans are coming," said Mrs. Arthur Heldreth of Shinns Run, just outside of town. Nearby, farmer Arthur Atkinson also initially thought the town was being bombarded from the air. He listened as his roof was pulled free from the house frame, then watched his kitchen door bulge impossibly outward before exploding into thousands of splinters. After the twister passed, Atkinson discovered that his pigpen was destroyed but its four resident hogs were unhurt; his barn was demolished, but his milk cow was left foraging in its ruins; and twenty-six of his twenty-seven chickens were unscathed, except for being stripped of their feathers.

In the Grangeville community west of Shinnston, eighty-year-old Cena Mason was found unhurt, sitting in her easy chair, surrounded by the kindling-like wreckage of her otherwise demolished home. Rufus Taylor, a telephone company supervisor, was assessing damage on the outskirts of Shinnston when he came across a refrigerator standing alone in a field which contained a dressed chicken, some ice cubes, and a large unbroken glass cake plate.

As the tornado swept eastward into Barbour County, a farmer north of Philippi reported seeing ten of his sheep being sucked into the funnel, and then deposited unharmed four hundred feet away on the far side of a dry creek channel.

While the funnel cloud dissipated after reaching the mountains east of Montrose, wind from the storm continued to carry debris from the Shinnston area eastward. In the days and weeks following the tornado, storm debris was found more than one hundred miles away in Virginia and West Virginia's Eastern Panhandle. Robert Hoffman of Brightwood, Virginia, 225 miles to the east, found a twenty-five-dollar war bond owned by a Shinnston man who died in the storm. Sloan Pearson of Moorefield, West Virginia, about one hundred miles to the east, found an assortment of checks, tax receipts, photos, letters, and a poem, all of which traveled by air from homes in Shinnston.

The Shinnston Tornado was one of four that struck the region on June 29, 1944, including one that first touched down near Wellsburg in West Virginia's Northern Panhandle and swept through corners of Pennsylvania and Maryland before re-entering West Virginia at Thomas, where it killed three and caused extensive damage.

Civil Defense emergency preparation training, in effect as a response to America's role in World War II, was credited with keeping the tornado's death toll from climbing higher. State Police and National Guard forces, Red Cross teams, and prison work crews were marshaled quickly from across the state to respond to the disaster.

Tornado experts have rated the Shinnston Tornado an F-4 storm, the National Weather Service's second highest category in terms of energy released. Although largely unknown or forgotten, the twister is ranked the fourteenth deadliest tornado in US history.

RED SCARE BORN IN WHEELING

1950

US Senator Joseph R. McCarthy's political future was questionable when he got off a Capital Airlines flight from Washington at Wheeling's hilltop Stifel Airport on February 8, 1950, and was greeted by former West Virginia Congressman Francis J. Love. Prior to his appearance in Wheeling, McCarthy's three-year tenure in the Senate had been lackluster at best. In fact, the US Senate press corps had recently voted him the worst US senator in office.

But by the time the junior Republican senator from Wisconsin left Wheeling the following evening, his name would be known across the nation, and his zealous anti-communist crusade, later to be known as the Red Scare, or McCarthyism, would spread like wildfire, claiming victims from all walks of life. He would remain in the glare of an international spotlight for the next four years.

The unlikely venue for the birth of the Red Scare was the annual Lincoln Day banquet, a fund-raiser hosted by the Ohio County Republican Women's Club. About 275 Republican women and men gathered in the Colonnade Room of the McClure Hotel in downtown Wheeling on February 9 to take part in the event, during which McCarthy would deliver the keynote speech. The McClure, nearly one hundred years old at the time, had served as host to such Civil War generals as Ulysses S. Grant, William Rosecrans, William Tecumseh Sherman, and John C. Fremont, as well as actresses Sarah Bernhardt and Jenny Lind.

McCarthy had prepared a speech on housing that he was considering giving during the Wheeling appearance. But Love urged him to give his hometown crowd another prepared speech with a spicier topic—the dangers of communism's spread.

After he was introduced to the crowd, McCarthy was off and running, blaming America's lack of success in checking the spread of communist successes in the Cold War to "the traitorous actions of those who have been treated so well by this nation . . . those who have had all the benefits that the wealthiest nation on earth has had to offer—the finest homes, the finest college educations, and the finest jobs in government. This is glaringly true in the State Department. There, the bright young men who are born with silver spoons in their mouths are the ones who have been the most traitorous."

McCarthy then held aloft a paper, saying, "I have here in my hand a list of 205 that were known to the Secretary of State as being members of the Communist Party and who, nevertheless, are still working and shaping the policy of the State Department."

He went on to accuse Secretary of State Dean Acheson of "proclaiming his loyalty" to Alger Hiss, a former State Department employee accused of, but never convicted of, spying for the Soviets. Acheson, McCarthy said, "has lighted the spark which is resulting in a moral uprising and will end only when the whole, sorry, mess of twisted, warped thinkers is swept from the national scene so that we may have a new birth of honesty and decency in government."

One Wheeling lawyer who heard the Lincoln Day speech said McCarthy's allegations "did not cause a ripple in the room." During a question and answer session with the crowd after the talk, most of the queries from the audience dealt with Social Security issues, or Secretary of Agriculture Charles Brannan ordering tons of potatoes, eggs, butter, and fruits destroyed as part of a federal price support policy.

But after *Wheeling Intelligencer* reporter Frank Desmond filed his account of the speech, which included references to the list of 205 alleged communists serving in the State Department, his managing editor, Norman Yost, knew he had a nationally significant story on his hands, and phoned it in to the Associated Press bureau in Charleston. On the morning of February 10, 1950, details of the Wheeling speech appeared in eighteen major US dailies, with additional coverage added in the days that followed. McCarthy made similar charges in public appearances elsewhere in the nation during the following week, often changing the numbers of the State Department communists he said he had identified, and never agreeing to name them. In a letter to President Harry S. Truman sent the day after the speech, and in a version of the speech submitted to the Congressional Record ten days later, McCarthy set the number of State Department "traitorous communists" at fifty-seven. Although he displayed what he purported to be his list of communists at Wheeling and other speech locales, he never made the list public.

McCarthy's Red Scare campaign struck a chord with a nation worried over the spread of communism in Europe and Asia and willing to believe that in America, communists had infiltrated the government, the entertainment industry, the media, higher education, and professional sports. Many authors, actors, athletes, politicians, and musicians were paraded before Congressional committees, where their political affiliations were questioned and their personal matters aired. Many people lost their jobs due to accusations of connections to left-wing politics and were unable to be rehired elsewhere due to secret blacklisting.

Among West Virginians who fell victim to McCarthyism's anti-communist frenzy was Fairmont State College art department chairwoman Luella Mundel, who, in 1951, publicly challenged an American Legion assertion made during an "Americanism" rally in Fairmont, that colleges were havens for communists. Within a matter of weeks, the state's higher education board voted not to renew her teaching contract after board member Thelma Loudin of Fairmont described Mundel as a "poor security risk" during a board meeting. Mundel filed a slander suit against Loudin, but lost. Fairmont State President George Hand, who defended Mundel to the higher education board, was also fired, as was a librarian who conducted a fund-raising drive on Mundel's behalf.

The Republicans rolled to a huge victory in the 1950 elections, and McCarthy was reelected to the Senate in 1952. McCarthy staged a variety of anti-communist hearings until 1954, when he recklessly accused the US Army of harboring communists. McCarthy's approval ratings plummeted after the Army-McCarthy hearings were aired nationally via radio and the public heard the way he badgered and interrupted witnesses. Despite countless hearings, speeches, and allegations, McCarthy failed to ferret out a single communist in the federal government.

Although McCarthy died in 1957, his name lives on as a synonym for witch hunts and groundless accusations.

DOWN-HOME DOWNHILL

1951

After an almost snowless winter in the east during the winter of 1949–'50, Hal Leich and Gorman Young, founding members of the Ski Club of Washington, DC, went searching for snow in the Allegheny highlands of West Virginia in February of 1951.

At that time, the three-hundred-member ski club made use of a portable rope tow that could be carried in the trunk of a car for use at snowy locations when they could be found within easy driving distance of the nation's capital. On rare occasions, the club was able to use the rope tow in Washington's Rock Creek Park. Otherwise, they organized train trips to the western United States or Canada, or held weekend outings in hilly Pennsylvania farm country when the snow gods cooperated.

Tired of having an unreliable supply of snow on which to plan outings and races, Leich and Young decided to try an unlikely expedition south of the Mason-Dixon Line to see what West Virginia, where skiing was nonexistent, might have to offer in terms of snow. One account of their 1951 trip asserts that Leich and

Gorman had heard from pilots that a large sheet of unseasonably late snow remained visible from the air on a shaded section of the four-thousand-foot mountain forming the eastern rim of Canaan Valley. Another maintains that they made use of topographic maps, basic meteorological knowledge, and common sense to decide that Canaan Valley was a good place to prospect for snow.

Whatever the reason that motivated them, in February of 1951 they drove down West Virginia Route 32 and spotted a vast drift of snow along a slope of Cabin Mountain behind the farmhouse of Hobe and Irene Mauzy, and asked if they could sample it on skis. They liked what they found, especially when the Mauzys and their neighbors informed them that snow sometimes remained on the ground past the official end of spring. After spending the night in nearby Davis, they returned to the Mauzys' slope the following day, spent a few hours skiing, and signed a lease on the property to use it as a ski area for the Ski Club of Washington, DC, the following winter.

During the summer of 1951, club members installed a rope tow lift powered by an old truck motor, still attached to its chassis. They also built a warming hut and spent numerous weekends pulling stumps from the ski slope and setting posts used for the rope tow. The Mauzys and other local residents, including the mayor of Davis, chipped in roofing materials, tools, and the use of a horse-drawn wagon to haul supplies to the warming hut site. The project used up eight hundred of the one thousand dollars in the club's treasury, but it proved to be money well spent. When the rope tow began hauling its first skiers during the winter of 1951–'52, lift tickets sold for one dollar for members, slightly more for others.

During the 1953–'54 ski season, racing was initiated, lift lines were long, and plans were being made to add a second rope tow the following winter. By the winter of 1954–'55, the second tow was added and through the club, the ski area, called Driftland, was offering lessons to beginners and sponsoring a Ski Patrol. In February of 1955, the ski club hosted its first Winter Carnival at Driftland, featuring slalom races, a costume contest, a snowball dance in the Davis High School gymnasium, and a Blessing of the Skis ceremony at St. Veronica's Catholic Church. More than two thousand people attended the 1956 Winter Carnival, including Governor William Marland, who walked up the slopes of Driftland accompanied by a bagpipe band in kilts to officiate at the coronation of the Winter Carnival Queen.

The winter of 1955–'56 spawned the birth of a second Canaan Valley ski area when ski club member Bob Barton of Richmond began operating a twelve-hundred-foot rope tow on a drift at nearby Weiss Knob. By the 1958 ski season, the Weiss Knob Ski Area was operating two rope tows and a T-bar lift, while Driftland had added a third rope tow and a second ski slope along with a rental shop.

Not to be outdone by the expanding ski industry in West Virginia's northern mountains, a ski area served by four rope tows opened atop Flat Top Mountain on the Mercer-Raleigh County border near the southern tip of the state. Bald Knob Ski Slopes featured a network of trails on Bald Knob, a 3,400-foot promontory near the site of present-day Winterplace Resort.

While the growth of skiing in West Virginia was fast paced in the 1950s, it began to cool in the 1960s as other ski areas within a day's drive of the Washington-Baltimore area, mainly in Pennsylvania, began offering comfortable on-site lodges, bars, and restaurants, as well as extended ski runs served by chairlifts. "People did not want to ride rope tows, sleep in station wagons, and use outdoor privies anymore," wrote state ski industry historian John Lutz.

Driftland closed after the 1961–'62 ski season, while Weiss Knob closed a few years later, and southern West Virginia's Bald Knob hung on until 1969. Meanwhile, in 1965, the West Virginia

Department of Commerce, armed with funds from the federal Economic Development Administration, began pursuing plans to develop a state-operated ski area on Weiss Knob as part of newly created Canaan Valley State Park.

The Canaan Valley State Park ski area opened in February of 1972 with one double chairlift traveling from the 3,430-foot base of the mountain to the 4,280-foot top of Weiss Knob, giving skiers 850 feet of vertical drop. A day lodge with snack bar, tavern, and rental shop was built at the base of the slope, with overnight accommodations available at the state park's main lodge, about two miles to the west. A triple chairlift was later added, along with a chair serving the ski area's beginners' slope.

Snowshoe Mountain Resort, the state's largest ski area, opened two years later about sixty miles to the southeast, atop West Virginia's second-highest promontory, 4,848-foot Thorny Flats. Snowshoe Mountain now offers skiers and snowboarders more than sixty runs and trails, some as long as one and a half miles with fifteen hundred feet of vertical drop, served by fourteen chairlifts. A mountaintop village offers a wide range of dining, lodging, shopping, and entertainment options.

In 1976, Winterplace Resort opened on a knob atop Flat Top Mountain, a short distance from the site where Bald Knob Ski Slopes served skiers in the 1950s and '60s. Winterplace now offers skiers and snowboarders nine lifts and twenty-eight trails, in addition to two lodges and the state's largest snow-tubing park.

In 1982, a few miles north of Canaan Valley State Park's ski area, the developers of Timberline residential subdivision built a ski area on the west slope of Cabin Mountain served by a twelve-hundred-foot T-bar lift and gradually expanded the operation into a resort with thirty-seven slopes and trails served by two chairlifts. Timberline Four Seasons Resort now offers skiers and snowboarders one thousand feet of vertical drop and the longest ski trail south of the Mason-Dixon Line—the two-mile-long Salamander.

White Grass, the largest cross-country ski operation south of the Mason-Dixon Line, began operating out of Bob Barton's abandoned Weiss Knob ski area in 1981. Under agreements with the new Canaan Valley National Wildlife Refuge, White Grass maintains winter trails on Refuge lands, helping the resort boost its network of maintained trails to fifty kilometers.

Skiers from Washington, DC, and surrounding suburbs in Virginia and Maryland still account for the majority of skiers and snowboarders making use of the snow Leich and Young discovered in 1951. While West Virginia's highland alpine resorts average between 160 and 200 inches of natural snowfall annually, all make extensive use of snowmaking gear, making skiing possible from mid-November to early April.

While skiing was unheard of in the mountain state prior to the Ski Club of Washington, DC, taking an interest in the state, West Virginia now sells more than eight hundred thousand lift tickets annually.

RELOCATING THE US GOVERNMENT

1952

The Cold War may have been heating up half a world away in Korea and Eastern Europe in 1952, but in West Virginia's two easternmost counties, people likely worried more about a cold snap destabilizing the region's multimillion-dollar apple and peach industries.

It may not have seemed like it at the time, but two sleepy communities surrounded by the ridges, valleys, and orchards of Berkeley and Jefferson counties had important strategic value to emergency planners in Washington, DC.

As the Soviet Union expanded and strengthened its Iron Curtain around its European client states and prepared to test its first hydrogen bomb, government department heads began thinking the unthinkable: How to keep the wheels of the federal government turning in the event of a nuclear attack?

Long-range plans called for the construction of permanent, underground "Continuity of Government" sites in the mountains of Virginia and Maryland—and under a planned addition to the Greenbrier resort in White Sulphur Springs. But during the years when those shelters were being planned and built, temporary Continuity of Government sites were needed in existing structures located within a seventy-five-mile radius of the nation's capital.

Since the eastern tip of West Virginia's Eastern Panhandle met that geographic requirement, planners began examining government-owned warehouses, office buildings, schools, and hospitals there in late 1952.

After rejecting a series of structures, including a fish hatchery complex, the old Federal Building in downtown Martinsburg was selected as the relocation site for top officials in the US Department of Justice, including the attorney general's senior staff and the hierarchy of the Immigration and Naturalization Service.

In nearby Shepherdstown, Shepherd College, now Shepherd University, was selected to serve as the relocation site for the Federal Bureau of Investigation.

According to formerly secret files declassified in 2010, the West Virginia Department of Education approved the use of Shepherd as a relocation site in October of 1952.

Shepherd's role was primarily to serve as the relocation headquarters for the FBI's Washington, DC, field office, and a backup site for all key FBI and Department of Justice headquarters personnel in the event that the FBI's Quantico, Virginia, training academy became "untenable" as the main evacuation site.

But in 1954, a plan was discussed to make the college the primary relocation site for both the Department of Justice and the FBI.

"It would be possible to allocate certain buildings to Justice and the remainder to the FBI, thus giving us complete control of our operations, yet immediate proximity to the Department," wrote FBI official H. T. Harbo in a memo to Clyde Tolson, the bureau's associate director. "The location is excellent from the standpoint of other government agencies, being in a twenty-five-mile radius of Fort Ritchie (the Department of Defense's temporary relocation site) and seventy-one miles from Washington, DC. It has good roads, a railroad, and it is on the Potomac."

The FBI initially equipped the college with a "450-watt code radio station" and later built a fifty-thousand-dollar microwave telecommunications station on leased property on the outskirts of Shepherdstown to serve the emergency relocation site.

At one point, the FBI considered buying the 126-acre Potts Estate adjacent to Shepherdstown and using its mansion house—which now serves as the president's residence at Shepherd University—as a communications center during relocation drills. In the event of nuclear attack, a cable could be extended from the mansion to the Shepherd campus, allowing the FBI to take over the college on an ongoing basis, according to a 1955 memo.

As it turned out, no relocation drills were ever held at Shepherd. According to the memo, "the influx of government personnel into the college during a test would severely hamper college operations," not to mention breach security.

In Martinsburg, about ten miles to the west, two floors of a building that housed the federal courthouse and post office were designated as the primary relocation site for the US Department of Justice.

In the event of a nuclear attack on Washington, "all Departmental officials including the Attorney General would go to the Departmental relocation site at Martinsburg, West Virginia, where they would occupy quarters in the courthouse," wrote John Airhart, the Department of Justice's relocation coordinator, in another 1955 memo. After meeting with his staff in Martinsburg, the Attorney General would probably join the president at his relocation site, Airhart wrote.

Plans called for about one hundred "essential" Department of Justice personnel and their families to "occupy the Shenandoah Hotel in Martinsburg" in the event of an attack, according to the memo.

Relocation drills were held at the Justice Department's Martinsburg relocation center in 1955 and 1956 as part of a nationwide Civil Defense Administration exercise involving nuclear attack scenarios.

The 1955 drill, according to a *New York Times* article, "was the first civil defense test in which the government actually left Washington, and in which account was taken of the lethal and widespread effects of radioactive fallout. During that exercise, fifty-seven Justice Department staffers were sent to the Martinsburg Federal Building, where communications technicians and their gear occupied two rooms. That communications gear was in turn linked to a pair of ten-axle Army Signal Corps trucks parked on the grounds of the Martinsburg Veterans Administration Hospital, nearly five miles distant.

As it turned out, the Martinsburg area's Jim Crow laws, still in effect at the time of the drill, posed more problems than communications issues. Attorney General Herbert Brownell had "considerable difficulty in housing his Negro chauffeur in Martinsburg," according to a drill critique. The experience left Brownell "quite apprehensive of the response which the Negro chauffeur might get in the West Virginia area if there were motor trouble or if it became necessary for the chauffeur to perform some errand for him during the drill."

During the 1956 drill, another problem arose when five US Border Patrol officers were sought to serve as security guards for the covert exercise. Apparently, orders to appear in Martinsburg in plain clothes were not received by the Border Patrol officers, who appeared at the federal building in full uniform, towing two trailers bearing the insignias of the US Immigration and Naturalization Service.

By 1959, the Justice Department made a newly completed underground facility near Bluemont, Virginia, code-named High

Point, its primary relocation site. The site is now operated by the Department of Homeland Security and is known as the Mount Weather Emergency Operations Center.

In 1970, after federal court and post office operations were moved out of the old federal building in Martinsburg and into a new facility, the Federal Aviation Administration converted the vacant structure into a regional records center.

Despite its innocuous name, the FAA center operated in an aura of secrecy. In 1973, when the building, completed in 1895, was in the process of being nominated to the National Register of Historic Places, an architect attempting to tour it was denied entry on the grounds that it contained top-secret aviation testing records. After the FAA vacated the building in the late 1990s, it became the headquarters of the Martinsburg Arts Center.

After the community arts group began occupying the building in 2001, it became apparent that something besides records storage had taken place under FAA management.

A raised, carpeted platform with enhanced electronics fixtures and stairways leading off its corners, which the Arts Center staff dubbed the "Command Center," occupied the ground floor. Bunk beds took up much of the space on the fourth floor and part of the third.

Shepherd University's role as an emergency relocation site apparently ended by the end of the 1950s.

In 2011, after the once-secret Justice Department relocation plans were declassified, several long-time members of Shepherd University's staff and faculty were contacted to see if they had any information on the former Cold War role of the campus. A university spokesman agreed to search for records of a former Justice Department or FBI connection to the school.

No one recalled anything about the arrangement, and no records could be found.

ARE WE ALONE?

1960

Frank Drake, a twenty-nine-year-old astronomer at the newly opened National Radio Astronomy Observatory at Green Bank, a sleepy Pocahontas County farming community, awakened to the shrill clanging of his alarm clock in the chilly, pre-dawn darkness.

The time was 3 a.m., and the date was April 8, 1960. Despite the cold and early hour, Drake had no trouble getting out of bed and into warm clothes to start the day. After all, mankind's first scientific search for extraterrestrial intelligence was about to begin, and he was directing it.

While technicians and construction workers had begun assembling a 140-foot radio telescope at the three-year-old observatory, a less powerful but well tested 85-foot telescope had been up and running since February of 1959. The Howard E. Tatel Telescope, named after the Carnegie Institute scientist who designed it, towered 115 feet above the ground atop an intricate 210-ton steel superstructure and steering axis. Its 5,700-square-foot white parabolic dish antenna, topped by a 36-foot focus arm, gave a futuristic look to the new observatory, which occupied former pastureland and hayfields lining the remote Deer Creek Valley.

Drake, who joined the staff at Green Bank in 1958 not long after earning his doctorate in astronomy from Harvard, had been interested in the possibility of other civilizations living in the universe since he was eight years old. Shortly after arriving in Green Bank, he began calculating how far into space the eighty-five-foot radio telescope could detect radio signals from other worlds, assuming they were equal to the strongest signals produced on Earth. Drake's estimate of a ten- to twelve-light-year range put several stars much like the sun within reach of the Tatel Telescope.

"I thought I just might have the tools to find extraterrestrials," Drake said in a 2010 interview.

The Chicago-born astronomer first broached the subject of using the new observatory's telescope to search for signals produced by an alien intelligence during an informal lunch meeting of Green Bank's scientific staff. The get-together took place on a snowy late winter day at a nearby roadside diner they had sarcastically christened "Pierre's."

Drake's plan involved adding a narrow band radio receiver and a chart recorder to the eighty-five-foot telescope and targeting two relatively nearby stars, Tau Ceti and Epsilon Eridani.

Fortunately for Drake, Lloyd Berkner, the National Radio Astronomy Observatory's director at the time, was all for pursuing what Drake was to call Project Ozma, named after the fairy princess in author L. Frank Baum's fictional "Land of Oz" series. So was the Green Bank Observatory's director, astrophysicist Otto Struve, one of the few senior astronomers of that era who believed that the universe likely teemed with intelligent life forms.

During their lunch meeting at "Pierre's," the Green Bank observatory's scientific staff discussed Drake's proposal, shared suggestions on how to implement it, hashed over an observation plan, and came on board with the project. "So as the last greasy French fry was washed down by the last drop of Coke, Project Ozma was born," Drake later wrote.

A newly developed parametric amplifier that would increase the Tatel Telescope's sensitivity by a factor of ten was donated for use in the search by Dana Atchley Jr., president of Microwave Associates in Boston. The instrument arrived at the remote observatory in the passenger seat of a British sports car driven by Atchley's chief engineer, who installed it and taught Drake how to calibrate it.

By the early spring of 1960, all the new equipment was installed in the telescope and ready to be put to use, and details of an observation plan were hammered out.

When Drake's alarm rang in the wee hours of April 8, he walked groggily through patchy fog to the telescope, where the operator pointed the instrument at an angle at which the astronomer could more easily climb into the instrumentation container on the telescope's focus arm. There, Drake spent nearly an hour adjusting the parametric amplifier before climbing off the focal point and entering the control room at the base of the telescope.

From the control room, Drake and his crew pointed the telescope at Tau Ceti, the first observational target, set the receiver to its starting frequency, and turned on the chart recorder, tape recorder, loudspeaker, and tuning motor. Project Ozma had begun.

Since such a search had never previously been undertaken, Drake and his crew didn't know what to expect and spent several tense hours staring at every mark made by the chart recorder to check for anomalies. At about noon, Tau Ceti disappeared over the western horizon, and the Green Bank scientists pointed the telescope at their second target, Epsilon Eridani, and turned on their recording gear.

After a few minutes of uneventful observation, the chart recorder suddenly began jerking violently and rhythmically.

"We heard bursts of noise coming out of the loudspeaker eight times a second, and the chart recorder was banging against its pin eight times a second," Drake later wrote of the event. "We had never seen anything like this before in all the previous recording at Green Bank. We all looked at each other wide-eyed. Could it be this easy?"

Drake and his crew suddenly realized that they had no plan in place in the event that they actually received signals emanating from an alien form of intelligence.

"Almost simultaneously everyone in the room asked 'What do we do now?'" he wrote.

As it turned out, they never had to implement whatever plan they cobbled together. Ten days later, they again heard the same strong eight-beats-per-second signals coming from the eighty-five-foot telescope. But the signals were also being received with equal intensity from a small antenna they had stuck out the control room window. The signals were the result of man-made radio interference, possibly from a high-flying aircraft's radar system.

Project Ozma involved only 150 hours of observation time and only about two thousand dollars' worth of special equipment, and it failed to make contact with intelligent beings. But it sparked the imaginations of astronomers around the world and led to international interest in SETI (Search for Extraterrestrial Intelligence) research.

While the National Radio Astronomy Observatory at Green Bank uses its array of radio telescopes to study star formation, detect gravity waves, and search for pulsars, it was also used for SETI research until 1993, when Congress dropped funding for the NASA-sponsored program. While scientific luminaries such as Arthur C. Clarke and Carl Sagan argued in favor of continuing the program, Congress followed the lead taken by Senator Richard Bryan of

Nevada. Bryan argued that NASA's SETI program deserved to die, since it had failed "to bag a single little green fellow."

"Many people in government are baffled by scientific research that can't guarantee a result within a certain period of time," Drake observed.

These days, private donors, including Hewlett-Packard founders William Hewlett and David Packard and Microsoft co-founder Paul Allen, fund the bulk of SETI research, conducted through the nonprofit SETI Institute.

In recent years, hundreds of planets have been found orbiting nearby stars, and astronomers have estimated that billions of other Earth-like planets could exist in the Milky Way galaxy alone. At the same time, more than 160 molecules have been identified in interstellar space, including sugars, amino acids, and other organic materials that could be building blocks of life if transferred to temperate exoplanets, suspected planets located outside our solar system, by meteorites.

Today, there is general agreement among astronomers that life, and possibly intelligent life, exists somewhere in the universe. Light years of technological advancement has evolved since Project Ozma began the world's first SETI search, making it possible for broader expanses of the universe to be searched far more rapidly and efficiently.

During a visit to NRAO Green Bank in 2010 to commemorate the fiftieth anniversary of Project Ozma, Drake used the observatory's one-hundred-meter Green Bank Telescope—the world's largest fully steerable radio telescope—to repeat his 1960 star search.

"The first search took two months," Drake said. "We duplicated it in two seconds, and the data were of a much higher quality."

Frank Drake continues to search for signs of intelligent life elsewhere in the universe as a researcher with the SETI Institute, a private research organization that operates the Allen Telescope Array—a network of forty-two linked radio telescopes in Northern California. Drake and the SETI Institute are using the ATA to study some of the 2,321 exoplanet candidates detected by NASA's Kepler space telescope.

A PLACE OF WARSHIPS

1964

Although it takes a river journey of more than one thousand miles to reach the nearest seaport, the lack of a nearby ocean didn't stop the employees of the Marietta Manufacturing Company from producing more than seventy seagoing military vessels during the shipyard's fifty-five years of operation.

While towboats, tugs, and barges were Marietta Manufacturing's specialty, the company also produced Navy mine layers and Coast Guard cutters that saw combat during World War II, and armed landing craft that carried troops and supplies during the Vietnam War. Later the shipyard launched a series of marine research ships for the Navy and the National Oceanic and Atmospheric Administration.

Marietta Manufacturing relocated to Point Pleasant in 1915 after narrowly escaping destruction from flooding in its namesake city of Marietta, Ohio, two years prior. The company bought a forty-two-acre tract known as "The Heights" on a high bank of the Ohio River and equipped it with a railway, dry dock, foundry, and launching facilities.

The company entered a boom period during World War II when production was shifted from the construction of commercial river vessels to seagoing military watercraft, including Navy and Coast Guard patrol vessels, mine planters, and net layers to protect harbors from enemy submarines.

"At one point, the workers here were building a new mine planter every sixteen days," said Jack Fowler, director of the Point Pleasant River Museum, whose father was once Marietta Manufacturing's production superintendent. "Between eighteen hundred and two thousand people worked at Marietta Manufacturing during World War II. When a shift change rolled around, the streets of Point Pleasant turned into one big traffic jam."

During World War II, the number of workers needed to operate the fast-growing shipyard and a nearby plant that produced TNT stretched Point Pleasant's housing capacity to the limits. By the time the government had contracted to build 350 new one-story, two-bedroom homes near each of the plants, some workers were being housed in a dormitory in what was once the showroom of a Point Pleasant car dealership.

Work on warships at Marietta Manufacturing actually began prior to the outbreak of World War II hostilities. In 1934, the shipyard built four submarine chasers for the Coast Guard. In 1941, during the months leading up to the December 7 Japanese attack on Pearl Harbor, the plant launched four Navy net layers that were used to prevent enemy subs from entering Allied ports.

The USS *Nike* and the USS *Nemesis,* two of the four sub chasers launched at Point Pleasant, were transferred from the Coast Guard to the Navy a month before the United States entered World War II. In early 1942, they accounted for two-thirds of the Navy force assigned to protect the Florida coast, as well as the waters surrounding Cuba and the Bahamas and a stretch of the Gulf of Mexico, from German U-boats.

Later in 1942, while patrolling off the coast of Delaware, the crew of the *Nike* rescued forty survivors of a torpedoed freighter. A few days later, off the coast of Maryland, they rescued the entire thirty-eight-man crew of an American tanker sunk by a German submarine.

In the summer of 1942, the crew of the *Nemesis* also had their hands full while operating off Florida's Gulf Coast. In addition to rescuing fifty-five survivors from a pair of torpedoed tankers, they launched attacks on five Nazi submarines.

Meanwhile, back in Point Pleasant, workers at the shipyard cranked out sixteen mine planters by the end of 1942, and in 1943 and 1944 produced more than fifty seagoing tugs for the US Army, most of which deployed to Europe as freight handlers. Enemy mines sank two of the Point Pleasant–built seagoing tugs—one went down off the coast of Sardinia in the Mediterranean in 1944 and the other was destroyed off the coast of Korea in 1950 during the Korean War.

Eleven 120-foot Landing Craft Utility vessels were produced by Marietta Manufacturing during the closing months of the Korean War, but most of them did not see combat until the Vietnam War, when they carried troops and supplies throughout South Vietnam's river system as part of America's "Brown Water Navy."

In the 1960s, the shipyard turned its attention to oceanic research and survey ships, and produced the five largest vessels ever launched at the Ohio River facility.

The National Oceanic and Atmospheric Administration survey ships *Peirce* and *Whiting* were launched in 1963. The 163-foot-long ships and their thirty-person crews traveled the world for most of the next forty years for NOAA.

During its career with NOAA, the *Whiting* produced underwater charts and maps from Lake Superior to the Coast of Honduras. In 1999, using high-resolution side-scan sonar, the vessel found the wreckage of the private aircraft in which John F. Kennedy Jr. and his wife perished while en route to Martha's Vineyard. On October 31 of that year, the vessel located the wreckage of Egypt Air Flight 990 that crashed with 217 passengers aboard south of Nantucket Island. In 2001, at the request of NOAA's Office of Ocean Exploration, the *Whiting* discovered the remains of the USS *S-Five*, a World War I–era submarine missing since it was reported sinking off the New Jersey coast in 1920.

The *Whiting* was decommissioned by NOAA in 2003, and in 2005 was transferred to the Mexican Navy, where it is now the survey vessel *Rio Tuxpan*.

The *Peirce* served with NOAA's research fleet until 1992 and was later purchased and used as a floating classroom by the Intrepid Sea, Air and Space Museum in New York Harbor. In 2011, the vessel was sold as a private yacht to an organization in Tampa, Florida.

The final oceangoing vessel built at the Point Pleasant shipyard was the Navy research ship *Kellar*, the last of three 209-foot ships produced for conducting experiments in underwater sound propagation.

Launched on July 30, 1964, the *Kellar* encountered a series of setbacks. Just after the ship arrived in New Orleans in September of 1965 for final outfitting, Hurricane Betsy struck.

"*Kellar*, recently delivered by contractor unfinished and un-manned, hit by one of many drifting merchantmen and torn loose from moorings," the commandant of the Eighth Naval District said in a message to the Chief of Naval Operations on September 10, 1965. "Unable to locate, as yet."

The *Kellar* was found overturned and drifting the following day, and during the next three years underwent an extensive salvage process. It was eventually rehabilitated and delivered to the Navy in 1969. After an apparently uneventful career, the ship was transferred to the Portuguese Navy in 1973, serving in its research fleet until its retirement in 2001. In 2012, the West Virginia–built ship joined three other Portuguese Navy hulks that were deliberately sunk to the bottom of the ocean off Alvor, Portugal, as part of a plan to attract wreck-diving scuba divers to the area.

Marietta Manufacturing's shipyard operation ground to a halt three years after the *Kellar* was launched. The company continued to perform maintenance work on inland marine vessels, but in 1970, the once-bustling plant closed.

In addition to military vessels produced at the shipyard, Marietta Manufacturing built thirty sternwheel towboats, four sidewheel dredges, fifty-three steam tugs, and six screw-driven towboats, many of which continue to operate along America's inland waterways.

Among former military vessels launched at the Ohio River shipyard that continue to operate are the World War II veterans USS *Nike* and her sister ship, the USS *Triton,* now excursion boats for Circle Line sightseeing tours in New York Harbor.

SILVER BRIDGE COLLAPSE

While crossing over the busy, two-lane US 35 Bridge spanning the Ohio River between Kanauga, Ohio, and Point Pleasant, West Virginia on December 15, 1967, Marjorie Boggs sensed something was amiss.

It was 5 p.m., and the towering suspension bridge, jammed with commuters and Christmas shoppers, had suddenly begun to quiver.

"What do we do if this thing breaks?" she half-jokingly asked her twenty-four-year-old husband, Howard, as they idled in bumper-to-bumper traffic on the bridge deck, waiting to return to their Gallipolis, Ohio, home after visiting relatives in West Virginia.

Before Howard Boggs could respond, a loud cracking noise echoed across the river, and one of the main towers on the Ohio shore began to twist and fall. In less than one minute, all three spans of the bridge twisted and collapsed, hurling thirty-seven vehicles and sixty-seven people into the icy river below.

The next memory Howard Boggs had of the event was of him breaking out a window in his car and scrambling out of the submerged vehicle. His wife and seventeen-month-old daughter, whom he could not reach, were among forty-six people who died in the collapse of the Silver Bridge, nicknamed for its distinctive shiny metallic coat of aluminum paint.

Several witnesses said the sound heard at the start of the bridge's collapse resembled that of a shotgun being fired, followed by loud groaning noises as the sections of bridge deck twisted and collapsed, like a deck of cards being shuffled, into the Ohio.

Onlookers, towboat operators, and rescue crews on both shores of the river responded quickly to the disaster and were able to save twenty-one of those dumped into the frigid water from drowning or death due to exposure.

One of them was trucker Bill Edmondson of King, North Carolina, who had almost reached the Ohio side of the river when the bridge "suddenly started falling sideways," he told a newspaper reporter. "When I got in the water, I got hold of a seat cushion, and that was all that kept me up until they pulled me out."

In the days that followed the Silver Bridge collapse, several local theories emerged regarding the cause of the disaster. One was that a sonic boom from a jet aircraft breaking the sound barrier had triggered the collapse. Although a number of people on both sides of the river reported hearing a sonic boom, conversations with military authorities turned up no presence of a supersonic flight in the vicinity on the date of the disaster.

Other even less scientific theories were put forward.

Some residents of the area theorized that the disaster was due to the "Curse of Cornstalk," named for the Shawnee chief who allegedly called for death and destruction to rain down on the Point Pleasant area in 1774, shortly after he and his warriors were defeated by Virginia militiamen there.

Another theory involved Mothman, the otherworldly winged figure with glowing red eyes, whose series of sightings in the Point

Pleasant area abruptly ended following the disaster, causing some believers to speculate that the supernatural being's absence and the bridge's collapse were linked.

A fourth theory, that a structural failure of a bridge component was to blame for the collapse, proved to have been correct.

The Silver Bridge, which opened to traffic on May 19, 1928, was the first suspension bridge in the nation to use an eyebar chain suspension system, rather than a wire-cable system. Eyebars are long steel plates with large circular ends through which holes, or "eyes," have been drilled. Metal pins, held in place with bolted cap plates, are used to link eyebars together or connect them with other parts of the bridge.

Each chain link on the Silver Bridge consisted of a pair of two-inch-by-twelve-inch eyebars connected by an eleven-inch pin. The length of the eyebar chains varied, depending on where they were used on the structure.

The American Bridge Company of Pittsburgh built the bridge to American Society of Civil Engineers standards, using a design created by the J.E. Griener Company of Baltimore. Ohio officials initially dubbed the bridge "The Gateway to the South," a nickname almost immediately forgotten in favor of the Silver Bridge.

By relying on high-strength steel eyebars, the design used for the Ohio River span made possible relatively lightweight, cost-efficient construction.

The 2,235-foot-long Silver Bridge was operated as a toll span by the West Virginia–Ohio Bridge Corporation until 1951, when the State of West Virginia bought the span for $1.04 million and removed the toll. The bridge was inspected in 1951, 1955, 1961, and 1965, and while several suggestions were made for improvements, the bridge was deemed structurally safe each time.

US Army Corps of Engineers personnel recovered bridge components from the river to make possible a scientific analysis of what went wrong. As it turned out, the expression "a chain is only as strong as its weakest link" rang true in the case of the Silver Bridge.

According to a National Bureau of Standards investigation, a tiny crack that formed while casting a steel eyebar later installed at the Ohio end of the bridge was to blame for the tragedy. Over the years, stress and corrosion allowed the crack to grow, eventually causing the piece to break through its eye and initiate the collapse of the bridge.

Once the eyebar failed, its pin fell out, disconnecting the suspension chain. The nearest bridge tower was subjected to an asymmetrical loading, forcing the tower to rotate and allowing the western span to twist and crash down on the Ohio shore, folding over on top of the falling vehicles. The span's eastern tower then fell westward into the river, along with the bridge's center span. The west tower was the last to collapse, falling toward Point Pleasant and into the river.

Investigators determined that bridge inspectors would not have been able to visually detect the eyebar fracture that caused the collapse without taking apart each link in each eyebar chain, or in effect, taking apart the bridge. The crack on eyebar #330, the bar blamed for the collapse, was only about a tenth of an inch deep when it went critical, according to investigators.

One factor that helped accelerate the corrosion fatigue and stress corrosion that brought the bridge down was the steadily increasing weight of vehicles using the span. The design vehicle used in planning the Silver Bridge was the Model T Ford, which weighed less than 1,500 pounds. The average weight of a family car in use in 1967 was 4,000 pounds. In 1928, the weight limit for trucks on West Virginia roads and bridges was 20,000 pounds. By 1967, the weight limit had risen to 60,800, and up to 70,000 pounds with special permits.

The Silver Bridge collapse served as a wakeup call for bridge safety across the nation.

Soon after the tragedy, transportation officials closed for inspection, and later demolished and replaced, the similarly designed St. Marys Bridge, now the Hi Carpenter Memorial Bridge, which crosses the Ohio River eighty miles to the north. President Lyndon B. Johnson launched a nationwide investigation to gauge the safety of America's bridges, eighteen hundred of which were older than the Silver Bridge. As a result of the Silver Bridge tragedy, bridge inspections nationwide became more routine and in depth, and engineers learned more about stress corrosion and corrosion fatigue.

Only one other bridge of a similar design to the Silver and St. Marys was ever built—the Hercillio Luz Bridge in Florianopolis, Brazil. That span, the largest suspension bridge in Brazil, was built in 1926 by the American Bridge Company—the same company that built the Silver Bridge. The Hercillio Luz Bridge remained open to vehicular traffic until 1988, when it was downgraded to use by pedestrians, bicyclists, and motorcyclists for safety reasons. In 1991, it closed to all traffic, but a plan to rehabilitate and reopen the span was under study and expected to be completed in 2013.

The four-lane bridge now carrying US 35 traffic over the Ohio River at Point Pleasant, completed in 1969, is named the Silver Memorial Bridge.

HARE KRISHNA, Y'ALL!

1968

It took a measure of vision to gaze upon a weather-beaten, century-old farmhouse surrounded by 133 acres of overgrown pastures, hardwood-studded hills, and vine-choked hollows in the middle of West Virginia's Northern Panhandle rust belt and see anything beyond hard work and headaches.

But vision was something Keith Ham and Howard Wheeler had in abundance when they arrived at Richard Rose's rundown family farm on the last day of March in 1968.

Ham, the son of a Baptist minister, and Wheeler, a college English professor, were two of the earliest American disciples of A. C. Bhaktivedanta Prabhupada, founder of the Hare Krishna movement. They met Prabhupada in New York City in 1966, not long after the swami arrived in America to spread Krishna consciousness to a largely unenlightened Western culture.

Three months earlier, while visiting his parents in upstate New York, Ham came across a copy of the counterculture newspaper *The San Francisco Oracle*. The newspaper included a letter to the editor from Rose, a seminary school dropout from the nearby factory town of Benwood, who had undergone a spiritual awakening and was living the life of an ascetic and yoga practitioner on his family-owned farm.

Rose wrote that he was trying to form an ashram on his land—a place "where philosophers might come to work communally together, or independently, where a library and other facilities might be developed."

While that much sounded intriguing to Ham, a final line in Rose's letter sealed the deal for a trip to the backwoods of Marshall County: "I do not think money is needed as much as determination."

For Ham, who arrived at the farm with seven dollars in his pocket, use of Rose's farm was the answer to a prayer. Prabhupada had spoken at length about his desire to establish in America a replica of Vrindaban, the seven-templed Indian city considered a holy place by all traditions of Hinduism. Ham, who was then on the outs with his swami for trying to "westernize" the New York Hare Krishna temple to make it more accessible to Americans, saw a Hare Krishna presence on the West Virginia farm as the first step toward creating the new Vrindaban envisioned by his spiritual leader.

After spending time alone at the West Virginia farm in the summer of 1968, Ham met with Prabhupada in Montreal, where the two settled their differences and reconciled. Ham, who took the name Kirtanananda Swami Bhaktipada after being initiated into the Hare Krishna movement and becoming one of Prabhupada's disciples, spent the rest of 1968 at the farm, joined by four other devotees. By the end of that year, they received a ninety-nine-year lease on the 133-acre farm from Rose for four thousand dollars.

In 1969, Prabhupada stayed at the farm for a month, urging its occupants to establish gardens and a sanctuary for cows, considered sacred by Hindus, and to build a school to serve the children of devotees.

By 1972, when Prabhupada returned for a second visit, scores of devotees were living at the nation's first farm-based Hare Krishna community, which had grown to encompass five hundred acres. The following year, members of the New Vrindaban community began work on a permanent home for their spiritual leader, choosing a ridge-top promontory with a sweeping view of the countryside. The site had once been an unofficial landfill for residents of the area, giving devotees an abundance of site preparation work to do before construction could begin.

Over the course of the next seven years, Prabhupada's Palace of Gold slowly took shape, often at the hands of community residents who were learning their construction skills on the job. The palace's namesake did not live to see it completed—he died in 1977—but during a visit to New Vrindaban in 1976, Prabhupada told devotees, "I'm already living here and always will be."

The completed palace, with gold leaf domes, crystal chandeliers, marble floors, intricate woodwork, stained glass windows, and ornaments, soon became one of northern West Virginia's top tourist attractions, drawing tens of thousands of visitors, many of them arriving on tour buses.

During its heyday in the early 1980s, nearly seven hundred devotees lived at New Vrindaban, which for a time was the largest Hare Krishna community in America.

The community's fund-raising activity spread nationwide, bringing in millions of dollars annually and attracting the attention of federal law enforcement officials. In 1987, the FBI raided New Vrindaban's offices and seized records. Swami Bhaktipada was expelled by ISKON, the Krishna consciousness movement's governing board.

In 1990, Bhaktipada was charged with racketeering, fraud, and conspiracy, and implicated in the deaths of two dissident followers.

The racketeering charges stemmed from the alleged sale of $10.5 million worth of caps, shirts, and bumper stickers carrying the unlicensed, counterfeit logos and images of sports teams and cartoon characters.

In 1991, Bhaktipada was convicted of nine of the eleven charges he faced, but the following year the convictions were reversed by an appeals court. As a retrial got underway in 1996, he pled guilty to one count of mail fraud and served twelve years of a twenty-year sentence.

After his release from prison, Bhaktipada moved to India and remained there until he died in 2011.

In the years following Bhaktipada's arrest and excommunication, New Vrindaban has rejoined ISKON, and its population of community residents is rebounding. It is once more a tourism destination, but not yet at the scale it once was. About twenty-five thousand visitors come to the remote spiritual community annually.

Many visitors to the community are members of the nation's Hindu community, who come to West Virginia's Northern Panhandle to celebrate festivals and holidays associated with their faith and view deities in the community's temple. New Vrindaban offers lodging in a lodge and guest cabins and operates a restaurant offering a variety of Indian entrees, as well as pizza and fries.

The community also operates the oldest cattle sanctuary in the nation, which includes an adopt-a-cow outreach program that receives funds from around the world.

A new hotel and seminary complex is planned.

New Vrindaban's current leadership plans to ride a wave of new natural gas development in the Marcellus shale formation into the future. In late 2011, the community leased its natural gas rights for $10 million.

TAKING THE PLUNGE

1979

At 10:20 p.m. on a hot August night, Burton Ervin of Cowen climbed a four-foot stepladder, stood atop a guardrail on the New River Gorge Bridge, and jumped into the 876-foot void separating the newly completed bridge from the rapids of the New River below.

After freefalling for nearly two hundred feet, Ervin deployed his parachute, which blossomed in the night sky, illuminated by spotlights pointed by some of the two hundred onlookers on the riverbanks below. Cheers echoed across the river as Ervin descended to a safe water landing in a pool upstream of the bridge and above an expanse of whitewater known as Fayette Station Rapids.

A coal mine foreman with fewer than forty airplane-assisted jumps under his belt, Ervin was the first of what would become thousands of BASE (Bridge, Antenna, Span, and Earth) jumpers to parachute from the New River Gorge Bridge in the decades to follow. He became fascinated with the idea of parachuting from the span as he watched it slowly take shape over the years in the county bordering his own.

While the jump may have seemed reckless to many, Ervin had spent months studying wind patterns and turbulence in the vicinity of the bridge and consulting with parachute manufacturers and riggers on the reliability of his gear. He had postponed three previously planned attempts when atmospheric conditions were not optimal and delayed his historic bridge jump until brisk winds and the threat of rain subsided after dark.

The New River Gorge Bridge, when completed in 1977, became the fifth-highest vehicular bridge in the world, as well as the longest single-span steel arch bridge in the Western Hemisphere and an eye-pleasing engineering feat. Its likeness appears on the West Virginia edition of the quarter-dollar coin. In October of 1977, to celebrate the bridge's completion, then-Governor John D. Rockefeller IV ordered two lanes of four-lane US 19, which crosses the bridge, closed for a day, making it possible for people to stroll across the lofty deck and take in the fall scenery.

Thousands of West Virginians took part in that "Bridge Walk" grand opening event, prompting Fayette County development officials to consider making an autumn day of pedestrian activity on the bridge an annual event.

"Bridge Day" became an annual fall festival in 1980. In keeping with the New River Gorge's identity as a region of high-adventure outdoor recreation, which includes whitewater rafting, kayaking and rock-climbing, a team of parachutists was given permission to legally jump onto, then off of, the bridge during the debut event. Early in the day, Ken Hamilton and Miguel Fernandez parachuted onto the bridge deck from a Cessna. As a climax to the day's activities, Fernandez, Hamilton, Dennis Wood, Andy McIntyre, and Bob Wolf became the first five BASE jumpers to parachute off the span legally.

Bridge Day planners expected about eight thousand people to attend the inaugural event. Instead, more than forty thousand showed up.

By 1984, as word of Bridge Day's legal BASE-jumping component spread, thanks mainly to an article on the event in *Skydiving* magazine, more than 350 jumpers took part. The BASE-jumping community established pre-jump clinics, checked gear, and weeded out thrill-seekers who lacked the expertise needed to safely make the jumps. Whitewater rafting outfitters and guides organized crews to pick up jumpers making water landings. State, county, and National Park Service emergency officials stationed paramedic crews, rangers, sheriff's deputies, and troopers at strategic points to handle medical emergencies and control traffic and crowds.

Bridge Day crowds gradually began reaching, and surpassing, the hundred thousand mark, while the number of BASE jumpers averaged about four hundred per event. Parachutists from around the world have traveled to Fayetteville to participate in the rare, legal day of BASE-jumping.

In 1990, the West Virginia Legislature passed a bill establishing a Bridge Day Commission to organize and promote the annual event. The bill also gave the state Department of Highways and the State Police the authority to close roads and reroute traffic as needed to accommodate Bridge Day activities.

Over the years, parachutists have exited the bridge from its railing, a sixteen-foot springboard diving board, a rope swing, a twenty-foot-tall scissor-lift platform, the roof of a parked bus, and a ramp. Landings have been made on boat launch ramps, access roads, trees, boulders, the river, a whitewater raft in the river, and the top of a satellite truck used to uplink live video images of the event.

While serious injuries are uncommon during most Bridge Day BASE jumps, despite more than eight hundred jumps sometimes occurring in a single day, there have been two fatalities over the years. While unfavorable weather conditions and river levels have threatened to cancel Bridge Day BASE jumping several times, parachuting has taken place every year since the event's debut, except for 2001, due to security concerns following the terrorist attacks in New York and Washington, DC.

Bridge Day has become West Virginia's largest single-day festival. On the third Saturday in October, anyone is welcome to stroll across the bridge deck and watch BASE jumpers and rappellers take the plunge to the New River's shoreline.

DUCHESS OF DUNK

1984

It wasn't the world's most exciting basketball game, but it wasn't bad—certainly nothing the one hundred or so fans in attendance thought would go down in the record books.

With twelve minutes remaining, West Virginia University's women's basketball team maintained the lead they had held over the University of Charleston squad throughout the game. But the UC women were closing in, trailing the Lady Mountaineers 83–80, as WVU guard Lisa Ribble in-bounded the ball to teammate Georgeann Wells at half-court.

The breakaway play left the 6'7" Wells unguarded. She streaked for the basket, soared into the air, and as the clock swept past 11:58, slammed the ball down through the hoop, becoming the first woman to dunk a basketball in a collegiate game.

"It was a planned deal," Wells said in a 2007 interview. "We had been working on it in practice so many times. We knew it was going to happen. We just didn't know when."

The scene of the historic slam-dunk was the Randolph County Armory in Elkins, host site for the 1984 Mountaineer Christmas Classic, a holiday tournament involving collegiate women's teams from across the state.

The WVU–UC game, which took place during an opening round of the tourney, received no on-scene press coverage, so there was no photograph of the historic dunk. The WVU athletic staff did not take film of the game for training purposes, so they had no cinematic record of Wells's achievement. The University of Charleston staff did film the game, but head coach Bud Francis, embarrassed at having his team be the first to be slam-dunked on, refused to make the film available to the opposing team.

While Wells was officially credited with slamming home the first dunk in collegiate women's basketball, the lack of photographic evidence of her history-making goal resulted in her achievement generating only a mild wave of enthusiasm.

Three games later, on December 29, 1984, she slam-dunked in a contest with Xavier, and the feat was captured on film. It would be ten years until another woman—North Carolina's Charlotte Smith—dunked a basketball in a college game.

In the years that followed, images of Wells's historic first dunk remained missing and presumed lost, somewhere among the possessions of coach Francis.

In 2009, as the twenty-fifth anniversary of the history-making shot approached, *Wall Street Journal* sports reporter Reed Albergotti telephoned Francis's son, Ford Francis, a Charleston attorney, to see if he knew the whereabouts of the game tape.

The younger Francis replied that he had no idea where the tape was. But after he got off the phone with the reporter, he remembered that a box of tapes had turned up in a storage room in a barn his father, who died in 1999, had used to raise horses during his retirement. He found the box, located the game tape, and called Albergotti back.

The *Wall Street Journal* reporter put a copy of the tape on a disk and drove it to Wells's home in her hometown of Columbus, Ohio, where he played it for her on a laptop.

"It was a really fuzzy picture, but you could see what actually happened," Wells said in a 2009 interview. "I was just like, 'Wow, that was me twenty-five years ago slam-dunking, the very first dunk of my life.' It was amazing."

Making Wells's feat even more amazing is the fact that she landed the dunk using a larger ball than the ones now in use by NCAA women. The ball she slammed down the hoop in Elkins was one inch larger in circumference and two ounces heavier than the regulation balls now in use.

Wells still holds the West Virginia University record for most blocked shots in a single game at 17, and career blocked shots with a total of 436.

HISTORIC HEIST

1987

Grocery store worker Harvey Stacy suspected trouble was on the way when he saw two men get out of a black four-wheel-drive vehicle that had just parked next to the Kermit branch of the Matewan National Bank and stride purposefully toward the bank's entrance.

Both men were dressed in insulated coveralls, which wasn't all that unusual for the blue-collar coal town of Kermit, especially in midwinter. But were those ski masks the men were wearing? It sure looked like it, Stacy thought to himself, as he made his way toward the bank's front door, which the two men had just entered.

Stacy, who carried a deposit pouch containing $19,074 in cash, checks, and food stamps from Kermit's Piggly-Wiggly Supermarket, made a mental note of the license plate number of the black Ford Bronco that carried the two men to the bank just before he, too, entered the building.

As soon as he entered the bank's lobby, one of the coverall-clad men pointed a handgun at him and ordered him to drop his bag and lie face down on the floor. As he complied with the demand, he saw the second man ordering bank employees to a fill a bag with cash from the vault and tellers' drawers.

"This is a robbery! Nobody is going to get hurt. The only thing we want is the money," announced the second man, dressed in green coveralls, suede gloves, and a ski mask, and also holding a pistol. The man who ordered Stacy to the floor only grunted as he kept watch at the door. He was wearing blue coveralls, a ski mask, and beat-up Nike running shoes.

For the duration of the robbery, estimated by Stacy to have lasted no more than three or four minutes, the supermarket employee kept repeating the Bronco's tag number to himself, in an effort to remember it in spite of his fear and anxiety. After filling a brown grocery bag and a green duffel bag with cash, the gunmen fled the bank and sped out of town in the black Bronco, taking with them $286,000, including Stacy's Piggly-Wiggly receipts.

The January 3, 1987, holdup was, and remains, the biggest bank robbery in West Virginia history. While the robbers made a clean getaway from the holdup scene, their future would soon be colored by murder, betrayal, and imprisonment.

The license plate number that Stacy memorized turned out to belong to a vehicle reported stolen the previous day from a gas station in Goody, Kentucky, just across the Tug Fork River from Williamson, West Virginia, twenty miles south of Kermit.

The two robbers—Russell Davis in the green coveralls and Doyle David Moore in the blue—drove the hot Bronco to a wide spot along Parsley Branch Road, a narrow secondary road a few miles outside Kermit. There, John P. McCoy and Harold "Boonie" Runyon, who planned the holdup, were waiting with a pickup truck. Moore climbed into the cab of the truck while Davis hid in a large enclosed toolbox attached to the pickup's bed.

The four men drove to a truck repair shop Runyon operated in Toler, Kentucky, twenty-five miles northwest of Kermit, along a route mapped out in December during a planning session at Runyon's garage. There, Runyon had showed video footage he had taken of the bank and the small mall in which it is located to aid Moore and Davis in making their getaway, and supplied the two gunmen with CB radios to use to stay in touch while making their escape.

When the four men arrived in Toler on the day of the robbery, they stayed at Runyon's shop just long enough to divide a small portion of the haul and go their separate ways. But their plans of keeping a low profile began to unravel almost immediately.

On the night of the holdup, Moore and members of his family traveled by taxi to Logan, where Moore paid $4,500 in cash from the $5,000 partial loot payment he received for a used car at a Chevrolet dealership.

That same night, Davis "borrowed" Runyon's pickup, drove it to Louisa, Kentucky, and then phoned Runyon, offering to buy the truck for twenty thousand dollars. Runyon, who was concerned tire tread patterns from the pickup could be traced to Parsley Branch and the abandoned Bronco, refused. Later, Runyon and McCoy, concerned about Davis's careless ways and propensity to talk about his illegal activities, limited his share of the robbery proceeds to monthly payments of five thousand dollars.

Within a week of the robbery, Davis traveled to Jacksonville, Florida, where he lived under an assumed name and bought a car. But federal authorities soon managed to track him to his new location for questioning about a crime unrelated to the bank robbery—the passing of fake hundred-dollar bills the month before the holdup.

When Runyon arrived in Jacksonville in late January to deliver another five-thousand-dollar monthly payment, he phoned Davis to set up an exchange and learned that Davis was at that very moment being interviewed by a US Secret Service agent about the bogus bills.

Back in the Tug Fork Valley, as Runyon and McCoy continued to hear reports that Davis had been boasting of his role in the holdup and other crimes, Davis continued to press the two men to give him his full share of the robbery proceeds in a single payment. Eventually, Runyon and McCoy had heard enough from their loose-lipped, free-spending colleague.

On a remote hilltop near Meta, Kentucky, about thirty miles southwest of Kermit, Runyon and his ex-wife dug a four-foot-deep hole for use as Davis's final resting place. A few days later, Davis, who had returned to the area from Florida, once more demanded his full cut of the robbery loot and arranged for another meeting at Runyon's garage. At the garage, McCoy and Runyon said they would square up with Davis the following day, if he would accompany them to a transfer site far from public view. The three men drove to the hilltop near Meta.

"Upon exiting the vehicle, Runyon shot Davis three times in the back," according to a US District Court narrative of the crime. "McCoy took Runyon's .22 caliber pistol and fired a shot into Davis' head. McCoy and Runyon placed Davis in the grave, removed his rings, wallet, and money, then covered the grave. The two then took Davis's car to Bluegrass Airport in Lexington, Kentucky, where they left it in long-term parking."

It took two years for the FBI to connect the missing Davis with the car in the airport parking lot, giving McCoy and Runyon time to move on to other criminal pursuits, ranging from counterfeiting to larceny to witness-threatening. After hearing reports that someone associated with McCoy and Runyon had been shot and buried on a hilltop, and realizing that Davis, a former associate of the two, was missing, FBI agents began looking for a grave. After weeks of digging, metal detecting, and eventually bulldozing, they found his bullet-riddled remains.

On January 25, 1989, McCoy, Runyon, and Moore were indicted on charges of robbing the Matewan National Bank branch in Kermit. Runyon and Moore were soon taken into custody, but McCoy remained at large until March 12. On that date, an FBI SWAT team arrived at a residence McCoy owned near Belfry, Kentucky, about twenty miles south of Kermit.

McCoy could not be found during a preliminary search of the house, but eventually, someone opened a kitchen refrigerator and found the cold, calculating criminal curled up inside.

McCoy and Runyon, who split Davis's share of the robbery proceeds after killing him, were later found guilty of bank robbery and conspiring to kill Davis. McCoy was also convicted of threatening four witnesses, while Moore was convicted of one count of bank robbery and one count of threatening a witness.

While in Cabell County jail awaiting their robbery and murder trial, McCoy and Runyon were charged in a plot to pay a third inmate $20,000 to help them break out of jail, kill witnesses, and escape to the Cayman Islands in an airplane Runyon, a pilot, owned.

Also charged in the plot was McCoy's twenty-one-year-old son, Kennis "Kip" McCoy.

McCoy was sentenced to life plus forty-three years for his role in the robbery, Davis's murder, the jail escape plot, witness intimidation, and the murder-for-hire scheme. Runyon was sentenced to life plus five years for his role in the robbery and murder. Moore drew a twenty-nine-year, three-month sentence for his role in the robbery and in intimidating a witness.

Kennis "Kip" McCoy was sentenced to nine years in prison for his role in the jail escape scheme. "I think you were sorely used by your father," said US District Judge Charles Haden during the younger McCoy's sentencing.

In handing out the stiff sentences, Judge Haden made it evident that the state motto, "Mountaineers Are Always Free," doesn't necessarily apply to murderers and career criminals.

WEST VIRGINIA FACTS
AND TRIVIA

- Kanawha County salt producer William Tompkins was the first person in the nation to use natural gas in an industrial application when he began burning it to evaporate salt brine near Malden in 1841.

- The world's first brick-paved street was a section of Charleston's Summers Street, between Kanawha and Virginia Streets, completed on October 23, 1870.

- Bloch Brothers Tobacco Company in Wheeling launched the nation's first outdoor advertising campaign in 1890 when it began painting barns adjacent to highways with the distinctive logo of one of its new products—Mail Pouch chewing tobacco. By the time the campaign ended in the 1960s, more than four thousand barns had been painted from West Virginia to Oregon. In 1974, surviving Mail Pouch barns were designated National Historic Landmarks by the National Park Service.

- Oakhurst Links golf club near White Sulphur Springs is the nation's first organized golf course, having hosted the first tournament on its nine-hole course in 1888. Since Oakhurst Links closed for several decades in the 1900s, Saint Andrews Golf Course in Yonkers, New York, justly claimed credit for being the nation's oldest continuously open course.

- The nation's first rural free mail delivery service began operating on October 6, 1896, in the Charles Town area.

- Mother's Day was first observed at Andrews Church in Grafton on May 10, 1908.

- West Virginia imposed the nation's first sales tax on July 1, 1921.

- Minnie Buckingham Harper of Welch became the nation's first black woman legislator in 1928, when Governor Howard Gore appointed her to complete the term of her husband, E. Howard Harper, who died while in office.

- The world's largest shipment of matches—twenty rail cars carrying a total of 210 million stick matches—departed Wheeling for Memphis, Tennessee, on August 26, 1933.

- America's first city-owned parking building opened in 1941 in Welch, then a bustling coalfield commercial center with limited parking space. The 232-car Welch Municipal Parking Building, renovated in 2005, turned a profit in its first year and is still in use.

- The nation's first federal food stamp recipients were the fifteen members of the Alderson and Chloe Muncy family of Paynesville in McDowell County. Secretary of Agriculture Orville Freeman presented the family with ninety-five dollars' worth of food stamps during a ceremony in Welch on May 29, 1961, to help launch the Kennedy Administration's "War on Poverty."

- West Virginia is home to the only federally designated wilderness area in which hazards facing hikers include not only unmarked trails and encounters with bears but also unexploded artillery and mortar shells. During the early years of World War II, the 17,371-acre Dolly Sods Wilderness Area in the Monongahela National Forest was used to train troops for the invasion of Italy. An abundance of live firing exercises occurred on the remote plateau sections of the tract. In 1946, an Army bomb disposal squad found and destroyed 193 live mortar and artillery shells. Since then, an additional sixty-six unexploded shells have turned up, with the most recent having been spotted by hikers in 2005. Signs at Dolly Sods trailheads and parking lots warn hikers to watch out for the munitions and to report their location to authorities.

- West Virginia has only one natural lake, tiny Trout Pond in the George Washington National Forest in Hardy County. The one-and-a-half-acre body of water has been known to disappear during periods of severe drought.

- Weirton is the only US city that borders two other states on two sides—Ohio to the west and Pennsylvania to the east. Weirton is found at one of the narrowest points in the state's Northern Panhandle, and its city limits extend all five miles from the Ohio border along the Ohio River to the Pennsylvania line.

- The world's largest teapot can be found near the intersection of US Highway 30 and West Virginia Highway 2 in the Hancock County town of Chester. It was built to draw attention to Chester's importance as a pottery hub, due to the presence of the Homer Laughlin China Co., which once produced 10 percent of the nation's pottery and dinnerware. The fourteen-foot-tall teapot, with a diameter that also measures fourteen feet, was built in 1938, making use of a huge wooden barrel that had previously been used in a Hires Root Beer ad campaign.

- The nation's first 4-H camp was established in 1921 at Jackson's Mill in Lewis County.

- Cecil Underwood is the only political figure to serve as both the oldest and youngest governor of a state. Elected to his first term at the age of thirty-four in 1956, the former high-school teacher was drafted to head the Republican ticket forty years later, at the age of seventy-four. In 2000, he lost a reelection bid to Democrat Bob Wise. Underwood died in 2008 at the age of eighty-six.

- On January 26, 1960, Danny Heater of Burnsville High School set a still-unbroken national high-school basketball scoring record when he racked up 135 points in a 173–43 win over Widen. Burnsville's coach urged the reluctant Heater and his teammates to break the state's individual scoring record, which had been 74 points, in order to increase Heater's chances for landing a collegiate basketball scholarship.

- The nation's first federal prison for women opened along the Greenbrier River in Alderson in 1927. What began as the Federal Industrial Institution for Women is now known as the Alderson Federal Prison Camp, which houses nearly seven hundred female inmates from across the nation. Inmates at the minimum-security facility have included television host Martha Stewart, Manson family member Lynette "Squeaky" Fromme, and World War II Axis propagandist Tokyo Rose.

- With 78 percent of its terrain covered by forest, West Virginia is the nation's third most heavily forested state, ranked just behind Maine and New Hampshire.

- West Virginia's holey-est county is Ritchie, which has been punctured by oil and gas drill rigs more than 11,300 times.

- The third-largest diamond ever found in the United States is the Punch Jones Diamond, a 34.46-carat gem found along Rich Creek in Monroe County in 1928 by William "Punch"

Jones and his schoolteacher father, Grover. During a game of horseshoes on the bank of the creek, the two came across a translucent rock they suspected was quartz. After keeping the stone in a cigar box for several years, Punch Jones brought the rock to the attention of a Virginia Tech geology professor, who identified it as a diamond. No other diamonds have been found in West Virginia before or since the discovery of the Punch Jones gemstone.

- When it opened in 1954, Memorial Tunnel on the West Virginia Turnpike was the nation's first highway tunnel to monitor traffic by using remote television cameras. Today, the tunnel, bypassed by a Turnpike upgrade, houses a mock subway station, terrorist's tunnel, meth lab, and a simulated collapsed parking building to train military personnel and first responders.

- West Virginia's only active-duty military installation is the Navy Information Operations Command base at Sugar Grove in Pendleton County. The base's stated mission is to "perform communications research and development for the US Navy, Department of Defense and various elements of the US government." Recently published reports have identified the base as a site for intercepting international communications for analysis by the National Security Administration.

- The longest and narrowest wildlife refuge in the east stretches nearly four hundred miles between eastern Kentucky and western Pennsylvania to encompass the twenty-two islands that make up the Ohio River Islands National Wildlife Refuge. Most of the refuge lies within West Virginia's section of the Ohio River, and the refuge's headquarters and visitor center can be found in Williamstown.

- From 1962 to 1992, a top-secret relocation facility for members of Congress was operated under the world famous Greenbrier resort in White Sulphur Springs. The 112,000-square-foot facility was equipped with thirty-ton blast doors, reinforced concrete walls, self-contained power and water systems, a decontamination chamber, crematorium, communications center, and cafeteria. US senators and representatives would have been evacuated to "Operation Greek Island," as the continuance of government facility was code-named, in the event of a nuclear attack. The underground facility was "outed" in a 1992 *Washington Post* article. Since then, one portion of the former bunker has been converted into a Cold War museum, while the other has been transformed into a casino for resort guests.

BIBLIOGRAPHY

California Dreaming—1671

Fallam, Arthur. *A Journey from Virginia to Beyond the Appalachian Mountains in September 1671.* "Annals of Southwest Virginia, 1769–1800," Lewis Preston Summers, Abingdon, VA, 1929.

Lauterstein, Ken. "The Ocean That Wasn't There," *Laker Weekly*, 2011. www.smithmountainlake.com.

Maslowski, Robert. Cultural Affiliation Statement—New River Gorge National River and Gauley River National Recreation Area, Northeastern Region NAGPRA Program, National Park Service, Boston, MA, 2011.

George Washington Soaked Here—1748

Mozier, Jeanne. "Archive of George Washington's Writings on Berkeley Springs," March 2002. www.berkeleysprings.com/GWarchives.

———. "The Early Days of Bath," www.berkeleysprings.com/bath.htm.

Steelhammer, Rick. "Where's George? Motoring Byway Puts You on the Trail of George Washington," *The Charleston Gazette*, March 19, 2000.

Getting the Lead In—1749

"Celoron de Bienville's Expedition." Ohio History Central: An Online Encyclopedia of Ohio. www.ohiohistorycentral.org/entry.php?rec=494.

Galbreath, C. B. "Expedition of Celeron to the Ohio Country in 1749." *Ohio Archaeological and Historical Quarterly*, October 1920.

McCulloch, Delta. "The Lead Plates." *Pocahontas Times*, November 20, 1924.

"Translation of the Lead Plates Buried at Point Pleasant." West Virginia Archives and History. www.wvculture.org/history/settlement/celeron02.html.

Bloodshed on the Ohio—1774

Lewis, Virgil A. "History of the Battle of Point Pleasant," Tribune Publishing, Charleston, WV, 1909.

"Lord Dunmore's War and the Battle of Point Pleasant." Ohio History Central: An Online Encyclopedia of Ohio. www.ohiohistorycentral.org/entry.php?rec=514.

Sturm, Philip. "Battle of Point Pleasant," *West Virginia Encyclopedia*, West Virginia Humanities Council, Charleston, WV, 2006.

Steamboat's First Test Run—1787

Beltzhoover, George M. *James Rumsey, the Inventor of the Steamboat*. West Virginia Historical and Antiquarian Society, Charleston, WV, 1900.

Dubose, Georgia C. "James Rumsey." *The West Virginia Encyclopedia*. West Virginia Humanities Council, Charleston, WV, 2006.

"Oft Encountered Inquiries," The Rumseian Society. www.jamesrumsey.org.

Woods, Robert O. "The Genesis of the Steamboat." *Mechanical Engineering*, April 2009.

BIBLIOGRAPHY

Thomas Jefferson's Lion—1796

Garton, E. Ray, "A Founding Father's Fossil," West Virginia Division of Commerce, www.wvcommerce.org/travel/ wvtravel4kids/funfacts/news/fossils/default.aspx.

"Megalonyx Jeffersonii Fossils," Thomas Jefferson's Monticello, www.monticello.org/site/research-and-collections/megalonyx-jeffersonii-fossils.

Spamer, Earl, and Richard McCourt. "Jefferson's Megalonyx," Discovering Lewis and Clark, August 2006. www.lewis-clark .org/content/content-article.asp?ArticleID=2742.

Steelhammer, Rick. "West Virginia's 'Official' Sloth Fossil on Display Near Cheat Lake," *The Charleston Gazette*, September 20, 2008.

Conspiracy Island—1805

Burke, Michael. "A Chronicle of the Life of Harmon Blennerhassett," *West Virginia Historical Society Quarterly*, January 1999.

"Harman Blennerhassett," Ohio History Central. www .ohiohistorycentral.org/entry.php?rec=41.

Linder, Doug. "The Treason Trial of Aaron Burr," Famous American Trials, University of Missouri, Kansas City Law School, 2001. http://law2.umkc.edu/faculty/projects/ftrials/burr/ burraccount.html.

Swick, Ray. *Blennerhassett Island.* The West Virginia Encyclopedia. West Virginia Humanities Council, Charleston, WV, 2006.

Tabler, Dave. "Blennerhassett Island: Staging Ground for High Treason," *Appalachian History,* July 25, 2011. www .appalachianhistory.net/2011/07/blennerhassett-island-staging .ground.html.

Whitewater Justice—1812

Marshall, John. "Report of the Commissioners Appointed to View Certain Rivers Within the Commonwealth of Virginia," 1816, excerpted in Virginia Canals and Navigation Society's *New River Atlas*, William Trout III, 2003.

Smith, Jean Edward. "John Marshall," *The West Virginia Encyclopedia*. West Virginia Humanities Council, Charleston, WV, 2006.

World's Longest Suspension Bridge—1849

Kemp, Emory. National Register of Historic Places nomination form, http://pdfhost.focus.nps.gov/docs/NHLS/Text/70000662 .pdf.

"Newspaper Reports on the Building of the Bridge," Ohio County Public Library History Online, http://wheeling.weirton.lib .wv.us/history/landmark/bridges/SUSP/bridge10.htm.

"Opening of the Wire Suspension Bridge Over the Ohio, *The Daily Wheeling Gazette,* Nov. 17, 1849.

Wingerter, Charles. "The Early History of the Wheeling Suspension Bridge," *History of Greater Wheeling and Vicinity*, Chicago, IL, 1912.

John Brown's First Casualty—1859

"His Soul Goes Marching On: The Life and Legacy of John Brown. A West Virginia Archives and History Online Exhibit." www.wvculture.org/history/jbexhibit/jbchapter10.html.

Johnson, Mary. "An Ever Present Bone of Contention: The Heyward Shepherd Memorial." *West Virginia History*, Volume 56, 1997.

Linenthal, Edward. "Healing and History: The Dilemmas of Interpretation," *Rally on the High Ground,* The National Park Service Symposium on the Civil War Online Book. www.cr.nps.gov/history/online-books/rthg/chap3b.htm.

Shackel, Paul. "Public Memory and the Search for Power in American Historical Archaeology," *Contemporary Archaeology in Theory: The New Pragmatism*, Wiley-Blackwell, 2010.

Philippi Mom Fires Shot Heard 'Round the World—1861

Daddysman, James. "Battle of Philippi," *The West Virginia Encyclopedia*. West Virginia Humanities Council, Charleston, WV, 2006.

Hanger Prosthetics & Orthotics History. www.hanger.com/aboutus/orthopedicgroup/Pages/History.aspx.

Lesser, Hunter. *Rebels at the Gate: Lee and McClellan on the Front Line of a Nation Divided,* Sourcebooks, Inc., Napierville, IL, 2004.

Swick, Gerald. "Fracas Before Dawn: The Battle of Philippi," *Wonderful West Virginia*, June 2011.

Statehood Stickup—1861

"An Important Military Post," Trans-Allegheny Lunatic Asylum, Civil War history, www.trans-alleghenylunaticasylum.com/main/history5.html.

"The Expedition to Weston," *Wheeling Intelligencer,* July 4, 1861, included in West Virginia Sesquicentennial Timeline, www.wvculture.org/history/sesquicentennial/18610630.html.

Steelhammer, Rick. "Seized Coins Helped Fund our Wartime Government," *The Charleston Gazette,* June 20, 2001.

Robert E. Lee Gets a Ride—and an Image—1861

Broun, Thomas L. "General R. E. Lee's War Horses—Traveller and Lucy Long," Southern Historical Society Papers, December 1890, Richmond, VA, viewable at www.civilwarhome.com/leeshorses.htm.

Lesser, Hunter. *Rebels at the Gate: Lee and McClellan on the Front Line of a Nation Divided,* Sourcebooks, Inc., Napierville, IL, 2004.

McKinney, Tim. "Robert E. Lee at Sewell Mountain: The West Virginia Campaign." Pictorial Histories Publishing Co., Missoula, MT, 1990.

The Golden Bough—1905

Carvell, Kenneth. "Clay County's Golden History," *Wonderful West Virginia*, September 2004.

Marra, John. "The Greatest Apple in the World: Striking Gold in the Clay County Hills," *Goldenseal*, Fall 1995.

Explosion Underground—1907

Linn, Turk. "Scenes Around Mines Just After Disaster," *Fairmont Times,* December 7, 1907.

McAteer, Davitt. *Monongah: The Tragic Story of the 1907 Monongah Mine Disaster, the Worst Industrial Accident in U.S. History.* West Virginia University Press, Morgantown, WV, 2007.

"MSHA: An Exhibit on Mining Disasters, 1907 Fairmont Coal Company Mining Disaster, Monongah, West Virginia." US Department of Labor. www.msha.gov/disaster/monongah/monon1.asp.

Roughing It with the Vagabonds—1918, 1921

Burroughs, John. *Under the Maples*, The Houghton Mifflin Co., Boston, New York, 1921.

Zacharias, Patricia. "Henry Ford and Thomas Edison—A Friendship of Giants." *The Detroit News*, Aug. 7, 1996.

Zumbrun, Francis Champ. "The Vagabonds End Their Two Week Vacation in Western Maryland," Maryland Department of Natural Resources. www.dnr.state.md.us/feature_stories/famoustravelerspart8.asps.

Blair Mountain Bomb Threat—1921

Ayers, Harvard. "The Battle of Blair Mountain Renewed," *The Charleston Gazette*, September 15, 2010.

"Blair Mountain: The History of a Confrontation," Preservation Alliance of West Virginia, 2006. www.pawv.org/news/blairhist.htm.

Laurie, Clayton D. "The United States Army and the Return to Normalcy in Labor Dispute Interventions: The Case of the West Virginia Coal Mine Wars," *West Virginia History*, Vol. 50, 1991.

Thornton, Tim. "Roanoke Proudly Plays Bit Role in Battle," *Roanoke Times*, September 3, 2006.

"West Virginia's Mine Wars," compiled by West Virginia State Archives, www.wvculture.org/history/minewars.html.

Training Airmen for Tuskegee—1939

Ledbetter, Charles. "Tuskegee Airmen: WVSU Connection," West Virginia State University History, www.wvstateu.edu/about-wvsu/history/tuskegee-airmen-wvsu-connection.

Rada, James Jr. "West Virginia's Tuskegee Airmen," *Wonderful West Virginia*, November 2008.

Sheets, L. Wayne. "Spanky Roberts," *The West Virginia Encyclopedia*, West Virginia Humanities Council, Charleston, WV, 2006.

Nuclear Dawn—1943

Jones, Vincent. *Manhattan, the Army and the Atomic Bomb*, US Center of Military History, 1985.

Proctor, J. P. "Production of Heavy Water at Savannah River and Dana Plants." E.I. du Pont de Nemours & Co. for the US Atomic Energy Commission, July 1959.

Funnel Vision—1944

Finlayson, John L. *The Shinnston Tornado,* The Hobson Book Press, New York, NY, 1946.

McCormick, Kyle. "Shinnston Tornado," West Virginia Department of Archives and History, Charleston, WV, 1958.

Lowther, Martha. "The Shinnston Tornado," *Goldenseal* magazine, Summer 1998.

Shinnston Tornado Press File, West Virginia Collection, Kanawha County Public Library.

Wills, Meredith Sue. "Shinnston Tornado," *The West Virginia Encyclopedia*. West Virginia Humanities Council, Charleston, WV, 2006.

Red Scare Born in Wheeling—1950

Moore, Greg. "Wheeling Speech Sent McCarthy on His Path," *The Charleston Gazette*, February 6, 2000.

Bayley, Edwin R. *McCarthy and the Press,* University of Wisconsin Press, Madison, 1981.

Desmond, Frank. "McCarthy Charges Reds Hold U.S. Jobs," *Wheeling Intelligencer,* Feb. 10, 1950, www.wvculture.org/ history/government/mccarthy.html.

Manchester, William. "The Anti-Communist Hysteria and the Academy: The Luella Mundel Affair." www.as.wvu.edu/ wvhistory/documents/097.pdf.

Down-Home Downhill—1951

Lutz, John. "Skiing From Top to Bottom: The History of Skiing in Canaan Valley," Canaan Valley Institute, 2010.

Lesher, Dave. "The Early History of Skiing in Canaan Valley." www.whitegrass.com/downloads/CV.ski.history.story.pdf.pdf.

Relocating the US Government—1952

Steelhammer, Rick. "Documents Shed New Light on State's Cold War Role," *Sunday Gazette-Mail,* Jan. 23, 2011.

"War Plans: Emergency Relocation Plan for the Department of Justice, 1954-56," 1966. www.governmentattic.org/4docs/ fbi-WarPlansEmergRelocatDOJ_1954-1956.pdf.

Are We Alone?—1960

Drake, Frank. "A Reminiscence of Project Ozma," *Cosmic Search Magazine,* January 1979.

Shuch, H. Paul. "Project Ozma and the Birth of Observational SETI," *Searching for Extraterrestrial Intelligence: SETI Past, Present and Future.* Springer Publishing, 2011.

Steelhammer, Rick. "After 50 Years, Scientists Remain Enthusiastic About E.T. Search," *Sunday Gazette-Mail,* September 19, 2010.

A Place of Warships—1964

"Cutters, Craft & U.S. Coast Guard Manned Army and Navy Vessels." www.uscg.mil/history/webcutters/cutterlist.asp.

"Marietta Manufacturing, Point Pleasant WV." www .shipbuildinghistory.com/history/shipyards/2large/ inactive/marietta.htm.

Skeen, Brocton. *The Marietta Manufacturing Company "History,"* West Virginia Historical Society, January 2008.

Silver Bridge Collapse—1967

Fields, Richard. "The Collapse of the Silver Bridge: NBS Determines Cause," National Institute of Standards and Technology Virtual Museum. www.nist.gov/museum/exhibits/ silverbridge/index.htm.

Grant, Sandra. "Now I Know What It's Like to Drown. Truck Driver Survives Tragedy," *The Charleston Gazette,* December 16, 1967.

LeRose, Chris. "The Collapse of the Silver Bridge," *West Virginia Historical Quarterly*, October 2001.

Steele, George. "Pt. Pleasant Span Collapses, 70 Vehicles Plunge Into River," *The Charleston Gazette,* December 16, 1967.

Hare Krishna, Y'all—1968

Fox, Margalit. "Swami Bhaktipada, Ex-Hare Krishna Leader, Dies at 74," *New York Times,* October 24, 2011.

Hubner, John, and Lindsey Gruson. *Monkey on a Stick: Murder, Madness and the Hare Krishnas,* Harcourt Brace Jovanovich, San Diego, 1988.

Ove, Torsten. "Obituary: Swami Bhaktipada—Disgraced Leader of Hare Krishnas in West Virginia," *Pittsburgh Post-Gazette,* November 30, 2011.

Taking the Plunge—1979

"BASE Jumping History at Bridge Day," www.bridgeday.info/ history.php.

"Bridge Day History," *My West Virginia Home,* www.mywvhome .com/bridge.

Duchess of Dunk—1984

Albergotti, Reed. "The Dunk That Made History," *Wall Street Journal,* March 20, 2009.

Garber, Greg. "Mother of Dunk Finally Getting Due 25 Years Later," ESPN.com, July 22, 2009.

Repanshek, Chuck. "What's Next for Wells? Behind the Back Dunks?" *Sunday Gazette-Mail,* January 13, 1985.

Historic Heist—1987

Hutchins, Frank. "McCoy, Partner Engineered a Decade of Daring Crime," *Charleston Daily Mail,* July 24, 1989.

_____. "When We Got to the Top, That's When We Shot Him," *Charleston Daily Mail,* July 25, 1989.

_____. "Trickle of Clues Later Gushed," *Charleston Daily Mail,* July 26, 1989.

United States of America, Plaintiff-appellee v. John P. McCoy, Defendant-appellant. http://law.justia.com/cases/federal/ appellant-courts/F2/944/903/34645.

INDEX

ABOUT THE AUTHOR

Rick Steelhammer is the author of *West Virginia Curiosities* (Globe Pequot Press). During his more than thirty years as a reporter and feature writer for *The Charleston Gazette,* he has traveled by car, plane, helicopter, raft, towboat, canoe, kayak, train, speeder car, horse, skis, snowshoes, snowmobile, ATV, mountain bike, zipline, and on foot to file stories from all corners and both panhandles of West Virginia. Steelhammer also writes a weekly humor column for the *Sunday Gazette-Mail,* which the National Society of Newspaper Columnists once judged to be the second-best in the nation among large-circulation newspapers.